CONTRIBUTIONS TO THE STUDY OF INDO-PORTUGUESE NUMISMATICS

CONTRIBUTIONS TO THE STUDY OF INDO-PORTUGUESE NUMISMATICS

J. GERSON DA CUNHA

Published by

Facsimile Publisher
12 Pragati Market
Ashok Vihar, Ph-2
Delhi-110052
facsimilepublisher.com

Distribution Network
gyanbooks.com
India, USA, Canada, UK, Australia, France

ISBN : 978-93-5324-535-1 (HB)
First Published, Bombay, 1880

2nd Impression 2020

Printed at: Gyan Press, Delhi.

**Contributions to the
Study of Indo-Portuguese Numismatics**
Author: J. Gerson Da Cunha

LAMINA I

CONTRIBUTIONS

TO THE

STUDY OF INDO-PORTUGUESE NUMISMATICS.

BY

J. GERSON DA CUNHA,

M.R.C.S. AND L.M., ENG.; L.R.C.P., EDIN.;

Knight of the Order of St. Gregory the Great; Member of the Committee of Management of the Bombay Branch of the Royal Asiatic Society; Member of the Royal Asiatic Society of Great Britain and Ireland; Corresponding Member of the Royal Academy of Sciences of Lisbon; of the Oriental Academy of Florence; of the Academy of Science, Literature and Arts of Lyon; of the Arcadia of Rome; of the Adriatic Society of the Natural Sciences of Trieste; of the I.R. Zoological and Botanical Society of Vienna; Fellow of the Geographical Society of Italy, and of that of Lisbon; Fellow of the University of Bombay, &c.

FASCICULUS I.

Bombay:

PRINTED AT THE

EDUCATION SOCIETY'S PRESS, BYCULLA.

1880.

EMINENTISSIMO DOMINO

CARDINALI LAURENTIO RANDI.

Postquam iterum civilis Europae praecipuarum urbium aliquas visendo, et summo gaudio numothecas earum scrutando,—inter quas insignem locum tenet Vaticana,—ad patriam reversus sum, aliquid temporis in rebus Indo-Lusitanis monetalibus discendis consumpsi, propter hujus speciei cognitionem imperfectam inter versatos in nummariis studiis.

Haud fere incepto opere, votum Eminentissimo Domino id consecrandi cor meum, beneficiorum memor amorisque plenum, me inspiravit.

In benignitate tua, tunc, confissus veniam impetro ad offererendum, princeps eximie Sanctae Ecclesiae Catholicae Romanae et doctissime antiquitatis investigator, hunc laborem lucubrationum mearum novo in curriculo primitias.

Accipe igitur, Eminentissime, opusculum quamvis nullius momenti, sed animi mei grati ingenuum documentum admirationisque profundissimae testimonium.

Eminentiae Tuae,
Omni fide et veneratione,
Obsequentissimus atque devinctissimus,

JOSEPHUS GERSON DA CUNHA.

Bombay, D. XXVII. M. Nov., A. MDCCCLXXX.

PREFACE.

Indo-Portuguese Numismatics have not yet been treated with that scientific method of exposition which has of late been bestowed upon other branches of Indian archæology. The reason of this omission is probably the difficulty in obtaining examples to illustrate, and in consulting archives to describe the subject.

To the rather fortunate circumstance of possessing a coins-cabinet, rich in specimens of this section, and of enjoying the facility of referring to authentic documents, hitherto preserved, on the minting of money in Portuguese India, from the beginning of the XVIth century to the present time, I owe the inducement to undertake to set down these notes. It is not, therefore, from any overweening sense of their merits—for, as the first attempt of its kind, they must, indeed, contain many imperfections,—but with a desire to fill up a gap in the history and archæology of the Portuguese in India that I have consented to their being brought to light.

One other reason, which may not, however, meet with general assent, for my pursuing these studies, is possibly the attraction or affinity said to subsist between the Sciences of numismatics and medicine. Dr. Teixeira de Aragão, himself a physician and one of the most distinguished numismatists Portugal ever produced, writes:—" Having spent the better part of life in dry medical researches, we dedicated, through analogy perhaps with the cosmopolitan science, the leisure-hours to deciphering some ancient coins, which chance brought to us. If the archæologist studies on the inscribed stone and metal the history of the generations gone by, the medical man investigates the working of the organization, inquiring minutely on dead bodies into morbid causes: with such, one reads the history of mankind with its rejoicings and long agony.

"Nature possesses, engraven by years, a majestic die, which shows designs that no burine can cut deeper."[1]

A similar mode of thinking must, indeed, have led Dr. Bernardin to publish, some twenty years ago, in Paris, his work entitled *Études historiques et critiques sur les médécins numismatistes, contenant leur biographie et l'analyse de leurs écrits.*

The subject of these notes is divided into four parts or *fasciculi*, the present being the first of the series, reprinted, with some additions, from the *Journal of the Bombay Branch of the Royal Asiatic Society*, before which learned body it was read last year. The second *fasciculus* is in the press, while the third and fourth are in preparation.

The first *fasciculus* deals with general observations on the institution of mints by the Portuguese in India, and with the description of the lowest of coins. The second treats of the description of successive issues of money in chronological order until 1580, the memorable year when Portugal became an appanage of the Spanish Crown. The third and fourth will be devoted to the elucidation of coins struck in the following 300 years, from 1580 to 1880, each paper describing in detail the coinage of 150 years, respectively. Every *fasciculus* will contain one or more plates of typical coins illustrative of the subject under treatment.

---

[1] *Descripção Historica das moedas Romanas do Gabinete Numismatico,* de S. M. El-Rei o Senhor Dom Luiz I., etc.; Lisbon, 1870, pp. vi. and vii.

INDO-PORTUGUESE NUMISMATICS.

FASCICULUS I.

THE subject of the Portuguese coinage in India is involved in much obscurity. Money was first minted at Goa in 1510 A.D., only 370 years ago; but its history is more vague and undefined than that of either the Greek or Roman coinage. The issue of coins by the viceroys, and often by the officers of the mint, without any intervention on the part of the viceroys or governors-general, was conducted in the most unsystematic, not to say capricious, fashion. The coins not seldom bore impresses, effigies, and legends which had no connection whatever with the reigning monarchs of the periods when they were issued. Some of them were still minted long after a new currency with crowned or profile busts of kings was introduced. Again, some of these latter coins were struck years after the kings whose busts they bore had ceased to live. These whimsical variations both in types and in the standard of money are in themselves enough to cause no little confusion in the study of Indo-Portuguese numismatics. But these difficulties are increased tenfold by an absolute want of examples of the early periods of the Portuguese rule in India, their place being but inefficiently supplied by some written official reports and private memoirs. The coins of the XVIth, XVIIth, and XVIIIth centuries are not only scarce, but even the written documents relating to them are rare or deficient.

Although the Mint of Goa was the first Portuguese establishment of its kind in India, four more came in course of time to be founded in their principal settlements of Malacca (or Malaca), Ceylon, Cochin, and Diu. The mint-master of Malaccá coined his own money, and called it *botelhas* from his name Nuno Alvares Botelho; and D. Jeronimo Azavedo and Constantino de Sá minted theirs at Ceylon without any regard to the standard or system of coinage prevailing in the mint of their capital settlement of Goa.

The history of the foundation of the Goa mint in 1510 is given at length in the *Commentarios do Grande Afonso Dalboquerque*, or

"The Commentaries of the Great Afonso Dalboquerque," compiled by Braz Dalboquerque, the natural son of the great Portuguese soldier and statesman, and first printed at Lisbon in 1557. As this work has of late been translated into English by Mr. De Gray Birch, and published by the Hakluyt Society, I need not quote the whole passage here, but refer only to the most salient points bearing on the subject.

Timoja, a Hindu chieftain of Onor (Honawar), who, being at enmity with the Muhammadan ruler of Goa, had just induced Affonso D'Albuquerque to conquer that city, went, in company with the principal Hindus and Muhammadans of the place, to the great soldier, told him that the people of the city, and especially the merchants, were suffering from a great depression from the want of currency of coin, and begged him to grant a permission for minting some money, and to order the price of gold and silver to be raised to prevent their exportation.

D'Albuquerque called a meeting of the captains of his fleet, and laid before them the request made by Timoja and the deputation of traders in the name of the people. The captains having observed that the coinage of some money should be commenced, the Viceroy replied that this being a novel proceeding—one that had never been attempted before in India—he could not venture to consent to it without first writing to the King, and with this reply dismissed them.

After a few days had elapsed, Timoja returned, however, with the same deputation, repeating his request in the presence of the captains, and praying earnestly that D'Albuquerque would either order a new currency, or permit the coinage of Sabaio, the King of Goa, who had already been conquered, to pass current, as without any of these barter of merchandise could not be effected. D'Albuquerque listened this time more favourably to the relation of the inconveniences resulting from the absence of some sort of coinage, and having again consulted his captains, who upheld their former opinion, gave orders for its issue on consideration that the King of Portugal would thereby gain credit, renown, and profit. Then, in order that the money should be produced in a befitting style, D'Albuquerque called a meeting of the goldsmiths and some Portuguese experts whom he had with him, Timoja and the principal men of the city, and commanded them to make a trial of the silver of the Muhammadan king. Having found that this silver was of the same intrinsic value as the Portuguese coin, the Viceroy appointed Tristão de Ga to be treasurer of the mint, where money in gold, silver, and copper were forthwith coined.

As soon as a large quantity of money was made, D'Albuquerque ordered that all the captains, fidalgos, and cavalleiros, all the noble persons of the fleet, the principal merchants among the Muhammadans, or Moors, as they were then called, and the Hindu *chitins*—more correctly *Sethis*,—all members of the trading castes in Southern India, either shopkeepers or merchants, should be called together. They assembled in a large hall of the Subaio's palace (wherein he used to live, and the ruins of which are yet discernible a few yards distant in front of the magnificent Cathedral of Goa), that had been especially decorated for the occasion, and D'Albuquerque told them that, having given orders to mint gold, silver, and copper coinage according to the arrangements that had been made, it was fit to make it public by proclamation being read to the people throughout the city, as was the native custom. The whole assembly having assented unanimously to this proposal, D'Albuquerque immediately gave the word to take the royal flag, trumpets, and kettledrums, to assemble all the men in the fleet, and commanded Tristão de Ga to go and proclaim it. De Ga did all as he was commanded: went with this multitude of people all round the city; proclaimed the minting of new coinage, and at each proclamation that was made scattered quantities in handfuls of the new money over the heads of the crowds, which were very naturally great, and eager to catch as many pieces as they could. And thus the proclamation of the first Portuguese coinage in India ended.

After this, the great Captain decreed, in the name of the King of Portugal, that from that day henceforward no one should keep any of the coinage of the Muhammadan king in his house, nor make use of it under severe penalties; but whoever had any should carry it to the mint, and get it exchanged for him with that of the King of Portugal's. The decree went on saying that whoever should break these regulations should incur legal penalties according as the Viceroy should think fit to impose upon him. "The people," says the historian, "were very much pleased with the money, and from that day henceforward they began to trade with their merchandise."[1]

These events took place soon after the first conquest of Goa, which occurred on the 17th of February 1510. But the city was retaken by Adil Shah three months after, on the 17th of May. D'Albuquerque hastened to win it back, and was successful in his second attempt on the 25th of November of the same year.

[1] *Commentarios*, Part II., XXV. The Hakluyt Edition; Lond., 1877, vol. II., pp. 127—131.

He had now to restore the order which, once established, had again been disturbed. However, he quickly arranged all matters. Amongst his new appointments held no mean place that of "a chief office wherein could be coined money of silver, gold, and copper, of the same standard which had been settled with the people and the merchants of the city when Goa was captured for the first time."[2]

He then commanded all the Moorish money to be brought to the mint and stamped with the dies of the King of Portugal, giving to the new currency the names it had after the first conquest. The mint was this time farmed out to a *Chetim* from Batecalá, at a rental of six hundred thousand *reis*, or nearly £125, Alvaro Godinho being appointed Treasurer of the Mint.

It will be seen from the above that only the coinage of the Muhammadan king was forbidden from being current, for the coins of the Hindu princes of Southern India were always in use in Goa from the day of its conquest to the time when they became rare. Among these may be specified the golden *pagodes*, now called *hûns* or *varâhas*, the former, a Muhammadan designation of the coin, the original meaning of *hûn* in Kanarese being 'gold,' and the latter, a Hindû one, of the emblem of the boar, one of the incarnations of Vishnu, adopted as the impression on their golden coins by the Râyas of Vijàyanâgara. The others were the so-called *fanaos* by the Portuguese, and *fanams*, or more properly *panams*, by the Hindûs, being gold coins of a minute size. *Fanao* was, moreover, the coin with which the Hindûs of the early days of the Portuguese conquest paid to the Admiral Vasco da Gama their tribute, as I have already mentioned elsewhere.[3]

Now with regard to the coins struck by Affonso D'Albuquerque, it may be remarked that there is nothing original in either their standard or in their nomenclature. He simply gave old Portuguese names for new coins, and minted them of the size and weight then in circulation amongst the natives of the country. He named his gold coins *cruzados*, this being the name found in the chronicles, but in contradistinction to the Portuguese cruzados of those days, they were eventually denominated *manoes*, in honour of the then reigning monarch D. Manoel "The

---

[2] *Opus ut supra*, Part III., IX. The Hakluyt Edition; Lond., 1880, vol. III., p. 41.

[3] An Historical and Archæological Sketch of the Island of Angediva. 2nd Edition of 1878, p. 11.

Fortunate."* They were probably meant to supersede the *pagodes* and *pardaos d'ouro* of the Hindû kings, being their equivalents in size and weight. They had stamped on the obverse a cross of the Order of Christ, resembling in shape the heraldic *cross patée*, and a sphere—the device of the King D. Manoel—on the reverse. As regards the value, each gold *manoel* was worth 420 *reis* Portuguese, while the pagode or *pardao d'ouro* was equivalent to 370 *reis, i.e.* about 1*s.* 6¼*d.* English money, the increase of 50 *reis* over the same weight of native gold being possibly aimed at as a restraint against its exportation.

The silver coin was equal in weight to a *brayani*, probably *brayan*, which in Hindustani means a partition or share, and is equal to two *vintens* Portuguese, each *vintem* being 20 *reis*, or a penny. These coins were called *esperas*, an obsolete form of *esferas*, *i. e.* spheres. They were probably called *esperas* in contradistinction to the gold coins called *esferas*, struck by King D. Manoel in Portugal, bearing on the one side the device of a sphere, representative of the sphere given him by D. Joao II., and now used as a symbol of the glorious acquisition to the Portuguese crown of the conquest of India and Brazil. On the other side it bore the Latin inscription *mea*, or 'mine,' intending thereby to prove the right he had acquired for it. But it also meant 'half.'

Then D'Albuquerque made another kind of coin, which was smaller, weighing one *vintem*. These he called *meias esperas*, or 'half spheres,' as they were just the half of the *espera*.

Lastly were struck copper coins called *dinheiros* and *leaes*. Now the word *dinheiros* (Lat. *denarii*, Fr. *deniers*) when used in the singular is a generic name for all kinds of money, and, although in this case it was used to designate a very small coin, it caused no little confusion and consequently they agreed to call the *dinheiros cepayquas*, a word still in vogue in the Portuguese settlement of Macao in the form of *sapeca*,

---

* *Cruzado* is a Portuguese silver coin now equivalent to 480 reis, or about two shillings English money; but formerly in the time of D'Albuquerque there were both gold and silver cruzados, the latter worth much more than now.

It is evident that what the English vulgarly call "pagoda" is but the "pagode," a name inherited by them from their Portuguese predecessors. What the Muhammadans called *hûn* هون for reasons above mentioned, the Portuguese called "pagode" on account of the emblem of the boar, to them an idol; while the so-called Ikri *hûns* with the legend श्री प्रताप कृष्णाराय (*Śrî Pratâpa Krishṇârâya*) were called *pardaos d'ouro*, or golden pardaos, *pardaos* being nothing else but a Portuguese version of the Hindû Pratâpa, as the Muhammadans had theirs of پرتاب or '*partab*.'

and the origin of which I have not yet been able to determine. The *leaes*, the plural form of *leal*, were a little larger coins than the *cepayquas*, three of which went to the *leal*. These copper moneys as well as the silver ones, had on their obverse impressed the Greek *alpha* supposed to be the initial of Asia, and on the reverse the ever-recurring sphere. All these coins had round areas.

To recapitulate the whole monetary system founded by Affonso d'Albuquerque at Goa on the 10th of March 1510, there were copper, silver, and gold coins. The copper coins were *dinheiros* or *cepayquas* and *leaes*. These were meant to displace the native coins of the corresponding size and weight called *bazaruccos* and *zoitolés*. Three *dinheiros* went to the *leal*—which was originally the name of a silver coin struck by King D. Diniz, and not a corruption or adaptation, as some writers have supposed, of the word *real* to Indian mouths, although twenty *dinheiros*, just as *reis*, were equivalent to a *vintem*. Of the silver coins there were the *esperas* and *meias-esperas*, the weight of the former being a *bargan*, equal to two *vintens*, and therefore that of the latter half a *bargan*, equal to one *vintem*. The gold coin called *cruzado* or *manoel*, meant to supersede the Indian *hûns* and *partabs*, was seventeen *bargans* in weight, and equal to thirty-four *vintens* in value.[5] It is said that d'Albuquerque fixed the weight of his *cruzados* at seventeen bargans (Port. *braganis*), in order that the gold coins should not be taken away out of the country.

The following year D'Albuquerque conquered Malacca, where was set up the second mint, with perhaps more pomp and circumstance than in Goa. The author of the *Commentarios* informs us that, having completed the building of the fortress in August 1511, inscribing over the gateway the verse of David, which says: *Lapidem quem reprobaverunt edificates*, an epigraphic record embodying the result of a strange and unseemly dispute amongst his officers, the great statesman was waited upon by a deputation of Ninachatu and the governors of the land, who declared to him that the people were suffering great inconvenience from the want of a currency, and begged him to give orders for some system of coinage. Ninachatu is said to have been a Hindu by nationality, who, having once treated rather kindly Ruy de Araujo, a captive of the king of Malacca, was by the latter recommended to the attention of Affonso D'Albuquerque. He was well received, and promised that,

[5] For further details of the coinage of D'Albuquerque the reader may refer to *Noticia de Portugal*, by M. Severim de Faria; Lisbon, 1791, vol. II., pp. 68—72; and a paper by Mr. B. Lopes Fernandes in the *Memorias da Academia Real das Sciencias de Lisboa*, 1856, p. 121.

before the General left for India, he should be rewarded in accordance with what Ruy de Araujo had said of him. And eventually he was nominated governor of the *Quilins* and *Chitins*, or merchants, who appear to have occupied separate quarters on the left of the city, having a palisade for their line of demarcation.

Affonso D'Albuquerque, at last, convinced of the necessity represented to him being urgent, and predisposed by all those motives which had induced him the previous year to found the mint of Goa, promptly ordered that all the merchants, governors, and principal men of the city should be called together, and, after holding a conversation and expressing many different opinions, came to a conclusion, agreeing in all with the captains who were then present, that a coinage should be made.

Now this system of coinage, according to the *Commentarios*, consisted in striking, out of two *caixes*, which was a tin or pewter coin of the king of Malacca, one with the *sphere* of the King D. Manuel, to which they gave the name of *dinheiro*, which is otherwise a generic term for "money;" the second, of greater size, which was worth ten *dinheiros*, they termed *soldo* (Lat. *solidus*, Fr. *sou*, modern Roman *soldo*, for five centesimi); and another, which weighed ten *soldos*, they entitled *bastardo*, the origin of which name may perhaps be drawn from some kind of Luso-Spanish coinage of former date.

Now all this money was of pewter or tin, which is found native in the land of Malacca, and the mines of this metal D'Albuquerque made direct crown property of the King of Portugal.

The King of Malacca had no gold or silver coinage in his territory before its conquest by the Portuguese, but trade was carried on by barter of one kind of merchandise for another. However, gold was coming to Malacca from a mine of Menamcabo, at the extremity of the Island of Sumatra, on the southern side, pointing opposite to Malacca, and from the kingdom of Pão. Only a little gold came from all the islands round about Malacca, where the Gores and the Chinese also brought it. With regard to the silver, it came from the kingdoms of Siam and of Pegu, where there were many mines of it, and its quality was as good as that of Castelete. Thus, though gold and silver were not made into money, they were both used by way of merchandise.

But D'Albuquerque ordered both gold and silver coinage; the former, a gold coin weighing a quarter of *tundia* (a native weight), and worth a thousand *reis*, to which they gave the name of *catholico*; the latter, also of the same weight, was called *malaquese*, according to some, and *malaquete* according to others, meaning 'Malacca piece.' And this silver coin was ordered to be made of "merchantable silver, so that if the Kings of Portugal should desire to send silver for sale to Malaca, on account of the high value it would fetch, they could do so."

Another historian gives a somewhat different version of the Malacca coinage. Gaspar Correa, in his *Lendas*, says that there was no gold nor silver coinage at Malacca, but that trade was carried on by barter of one kind of merchandise for another, while the eatables were bought at the bazâr by a coin of tin (*estanho*), which they called *calayns*. The governor, however, commanded a tin coin to be struck of a very low value, besides one worth ten soldos, to which he gave the name of *bastardo*, stamping on the one side the sphere, and a Greek *alpha* on the other. Then he issued gold coins of the value of a thousand and forty *reis*, bearing on the obverse the bust of the King with crown and a sword in hand, surrounded by the legend "*Com esta conquistada e ganhada*," or "with this conquered and won," and on the reverse the royal coat-of-arms with the words "*Gloria pera sempre memoria.*" To this coin he gave the name of *catolica*, and, after this, he got struck half or *meos-catolicos*, of the value of five hundred and twenty *reis*, bearing on one side the sphere with the inscription "*Espera em Deus pera mais*," and on the other the Greek A with the words "*O escravo ganha pera o senhor*," and these coins were handsome, of which a large quantity was issued. With respect to the silver coinage, silver pieces of the value of seven hundred and twenty *reis* were struck, called *reaes brancos* and *meos reaes*, bearing on the obverse the coat-of-arms of the kingdom without the crown, and on the reverse the sphere with the same words."[6]

Now, according to the author of the *Commentarios*, the scheme of Malacca coinage, when tabulated, runs thus:—

TIN OR PEWTER.

2 *Caixes*........... = 1 *espera* = 1 *dinheiro.*

10 *Dinheiros* ... .. = 1 *soldo.*

10 *soldos* .... = 1 *bastardo.*

SILVER.

Malaquese or *Malaquete* = ¼ *Tundia.*

GOLD.

1 *Catholico* ...... = ¼ *Tundia* = 1,000 *reis.*

According to the author of the *Lendas*, the scheme is as follows:—

TIN OR PEWTER.

10 *soldos* .... = 1 *bastardo.*

---

[6] Tome II., p. 256.

SILVER.

720 *reaes* .... = 1 *real branco, i. e.*, white *real*

GOLD.

520 *reaes* .... = 1 half *catholico.*
1,040 *reaes* .... = 1 *catholico.*

But to return to the narrative. D'Albuquerque gave orders not merely for the establishment of a house for the mint, but as well for all the Moors to convey thither without delay, under pain of death, all the quantity of money in their possession to be recoined; which was done, and in a short time coins in gold, silver, and tin were issued.

The Governor then commanded the merchants and others to be summoned, and told them that, having already minted a large sum of money, it was necessary to send forth a proclamation concerning it throughout the city with that solemnity which belonged to the estate of the King D. Manuel, his lord. In accordance with the resolution then come to, all the principal men of the place met together the following morning, and made their way to the fortress, where D'Albuquerque was with all the captains, fidalgos, and cávalleiros of the fleet. From this place they began the procession for the publication of the new coinage, which I shall quote in the words of the *Commentarios* themselves:—

"There went first, in front of all the people, one of the principal Governors of the City mounted upon an elephant with his castle caparisoned with silk, and carrying in his hands a flag of the arms of the King of Portugal upon a long spear, and behind him went all the people on foot on one side and the other, as it were in a procession; and in the midst of these people there went a Moor mounted upon another elephant likewise caparisoned with silk, making the proclamation; and behind this one came the trumpets; and after them the Governors of the City and all the Merchants and principal men thereof; and at the rear of this throng there went Antonio de Souza the son of João de Souza of Santarem, and the son of Ninachatu, both together upon a large elephant, which had been kept for the King's own use, with his castle caparisoned with brocaded cloths, and they carried with them a large quantity of gold, silver, and copper coin, which they kept on throwing out over the heads of all the people at each publication of the proclamation which the Moor made. The crowd was so great that the streets could scarcely contain it, and with many songs and blowing of horns, according to the native custom, the people gave great praise to Afonso Dalboquerque for giving orders for this distribution of money by the advice and in accordance with the opinions of their natives."[7]

With reference to the coin named *caixes*, we are told elsewhere, that the King of Malacca, called Xaquendarxa, who was a vassal of the Emperor of China, obtained permission to coin small moneys of tin or pewter, to which he gave the name of *caixes*, "which are like our *ceitils*, and a hundred of them go to the *calaim*, and each *calaim* was worth, according to an appointed law, eleven *reis* and four *ceitils*."[8]

Some writers say that two *caixes* or *caixas* were equal to three *reis*, that the Chinese *Le* (? Portug., *Re*) is the European *cash*, and that 100 *Le* are equal to 1 *candarim* (? Portug. *calaim*). *Calaim* is here the name of a coin, although the word signifies a very fine kind of Indian tin, and is used as equivalent to *estanho*; while *ceitil* is a Portuguese copper piece, which some derive from Ceita, and others from *sextil*, or the sixth part of the copper *real*. Of *caixas* and *calaim* I shall speak more at length in Fasciculus II.

To exhaust the whole subject of the Indo-Portuguese numismatics would take a series of papers, and it may be deemed advisable to leave for future contributions all that the successors of D'Albuquerque enacted, in continuing or modifying the gold, silver, and copper currency instituted by the great statesman. At present, I shall confine myself to one set of coins, the lowest in value. They are made of tin or pewter, and of an amalgam called *tutenag*, sometimes named Chinese silver, the *Packfong* of the East Indies. This is stated to be an alloy of zinc and copper, but the coins of tutenag minted by the Portuguese at Goa and Diu contained variable proportions of tin and lead.

The earliest notice of the tutenag coins, besides those struck by the Senate of Goa and the Government of Malacca in the early days of conquest soon after 1510, is contained in a written document dated the 20th March 1615. The smallest of them was called *roda* or 'wheel,' from bearing on the obverse a representation of the wheel of St. Catherine, the patron saint of Goa, on account of that city having been retaken by the Portuguese on her day, the 25th of November. The wheel was also a conspicuous emblem in the arms or skutcheon of the

---

[7] *Commentarios*, etc., Part III., XXXII. The Hakluyt edition; Lond., 1880, vol. III., p. 141.

[8] *Ibid.*, pp. 77-78.

CONTRIBUTIONS

TO THE

STUDY OF INDO-PORTUGUESE NUMISMATICS.

BY

J. GERSON DA CUNHA,

M.R.C.S. AND L.M., ENG.; L.R.C.P., EDIN.,

Knight of the Order of St. Gregory the Great; Member of the Committee of Management of the Bombay Branch of the Royal Asiatic Society; Member of the Royal Asiatic Society of Great Britain and Ireland; Corresponding Member of the Royal Academy of Sciences of Lisbon; of the Oriental Academy of Florence; of the Academy of Science, Literature and Arts of Lyon; of the Arcadia of Rome; of the Adriatic Society of the Natural Sciences of Trieste; of the I.R. Zoological and Botanical Society of Vienna; Fellow of the Geographical Society of Italy, and of that of Lisbon; Fellow of the University of Bombay, &c.

FASCICULUS II.

Bombay:

PRINTED AT THE

EDUCATION SOCIETY'S PRESS, BYCULLA.

1880.

Senate or Municipality of Goa, and I believe it is so even now. On the reverse it had stamped on it the Portuguese royal arms.

The *roda* was equivalent to 2½ *bazaruccos* of the original native standard of Goa. There was, besides this, the *duas rodas*, a coin double that of the *roda*, and therefore equivalent to 5 bazaruccos. Then there were the so-called *meio vintem*, being equal to 7½ bazaruccos, and the *vintem*, equal to 15 bazaruccos or 12 reis.

The later coinage of this curious amalgam had impressed on the one face the cross of the Order of Christ, with the date of the year of it, and the numbers placed in the angles of the cross; and the Portuguese royal arms on the other. This sort of metal being the most easily worn out, it is extremely difficult to obtain coins with clear and perceptible impressions, unless one can have the very rare chance of finding them under ground. But all these coins, whether old or new, are now out of circulation, and to be found only amongst numismatists or collectors of coins.

Description of the Coins.

No. 1.—This is the *roda*. On the obverse is the wheel, and on the reverse the Portuguese royal coat-of-arms. Its weight is grs. 40.

No. 2.—This coin is just twice the size and twice as heavy as No. 1. It has the corresponding wheel and royal arms as above. Its weight is grs. 80.

Nos. 3 and 4.—These are equivalent to No. 2, but are of the later coinage. There is on the obverse the cross of the Order of Christ, with the date and the royal arms on the reverse. Although the weight of each of them is grs. 80, one has a larger area than the other, indicating two different coinages, the larger from the mint of Goa and the smaller from that of Diu, where they are generally known by the name of *atiás*.

No. 5.—This coin is a very rare specimen. It has the Roman numeral VI., which means six *bazaruccos*, and the year 1769 below it on the obverse, and the royal coat-of-arms on the reverse. Its weight is grs. 100. The letters G-A stand for Goa.

No. 6.—This is the oldest tutenag *vintem*, of the value of 12 reis, found while making some excavations in an old Portuguese building at Tannâ. The obverse bears the wheel and the reverse the coat-of-arms. Its weight is grs. 270. The letters B-B stand for Baçaim (Bassein).

No. 7.—This is a coin of later coinage, having the cross of the Order of Christ on the obverse, with the date; and the coat-of-arms on the reverse. Its weight is 240 grains. Here, the letters D-D stand for Diu.

FASCICULUS II.

I.

It is nearly eleven months since I had the pleasure of preparing the First Part of this series, and I regret that my almost incessant professional duties have prevented me from following up the subject at a shorter interval. Still, some consolation may perhaps be derived from the delay thus caused having enabled me to collect more materials and to procure a few rare, and in two or three cases unique, specimens of coins to illustrate them. These coins, which the few numismatists who have written on the subject consider as irretrievably lost, have been found underground, some while laying the foundations of a house at Ribandar, one of the suburbs of the city of New Goa, and others amongst the ruins of Bassein, Tannâ, and Chaul, one having been brought from Supâra.

It was in the reign of D. Manuel "The Fortunate," under whose auspices India was discovered by the route of the Cape of Good Hope, and who ruled from 1495 to 1521, that money was first minted in Goa during the governorship of Affonso d'Albuquerque, which lasted from 1509 to 1515. This coinage was at one time current all along the western coast from the Persian Gulf to the Indian Archipelago, and in some parts of the eastern coast as far as the Bay of Bengal. It was originally meant to supersede the coinage of the Muḥammadan ruler of Goa, while the coins of the Hindû princes of the adjacent countries were admitted freely into circulation.

D'Albuquerque's scheme, like that of the founder of the Pathân dynasty, was avowedly adaptive. No historical parallel can ever be quite exact, but finding on comparison more points of similitude than of contrast, it seems that the central idea of the coinage of the founder of the Portuguese Empire in the East was analogous to that of Muḥammad Ghori. Both of them retained the mechanical identity of metal, size, and value of the coinage of their predecessors introductory to the more systematic mintages of their successors. Thus, while assimilating gradually, or without any violence, the issues of former Governments, and attempting to maintain the supply of the local currency, they proclaimed at the same time the conquest, the one by joining, as Mr. Thomas has shown in his excellent *Chronicles*,[1] the names of Muḥammad bin Sam and of Prithvî Râja on one and the same coin, the other by stamping new symbols, such as the cross of the Order of Christ, and a style of epigraphs, the first perhaps that India ever witnessed within her boundaries since the introduction of Christianity into the world. Thus the coinage of the Great Albuquerque was not only a fiscal necessity of his new government, but a Portuguese *Fatah-nâmah*, so to speak,—a declaration of his success as a victor and of his supremacy, designedly avoiding simultaneously all interference with the course of trade by any unnecessary monetary complication.

Now, before describing the coins struck by D'Albuquerque, some remarks may be necessary on the mints. In my previous paper the foundation of the first Portuguese mint in India was briefly sketched, and only incidentally five mint cities—viz., Goa, Cochin, Ceylon, Malacca, and Diu—were mentioned. To these I have to add three others, Damaun, Bassein, and Chaul. And, in considering the subject of the Indo-Portuguese coinage in all these mints, I believe it will be conducive to clearness if I take it up in chronological order under successive sovereigns of Portugal and their Viceroys in India, beginning with the first minting of money in Goa on the 12th of March 1510, and ending with the Anglo-Portuguese Treaty, dated the 26th of December 1878, which has considerably altered the currency of the country, bringing it, according to the 5th Art. of that Convention between the two allied nations, to the uniform standard with the British coinage in India. The Indo-Portuguese coinage thus represents 370 years of the annals of Portuguese India, a chapter which has hitherto remained unwritten to complete the history of the currencies of the Indian peninsula.

The subject is, however, so vast that the present paper can scarcely go, I am afraid, beyond a period of seventy years, ending in 1580, which is an important epoch in the history of the Lusitanian kingdom, when Portugal witnessed a dynastic change, the whole peninsula being united under one head, and that most unfortunately Phillip II. of Spain.

---

1 *Chronicles of the Pathân Kings of Delhi*, &c., by Ed. Thomas: Lond., 1871, pp. 17 and 18.

How different would have been the history of the Asiatic possessions of the Portuguese if that head had been the Duke of Bragança? But one must say with Ovid, *Sic erat in fatis.*

The Chronicles tell us that D'Albuquerque caused money in gold, silver, and copper to be minted in Goa. His gold coins were, according to some, called *cruzados*, and according to others, *manues*, in honour of the King D. Manuel, this name being again given to a tower erected in the city by the great warrior. The *Commentaries of Afonso Dalboquerque* inform us that all coins struck by the order of D'Albuquerque were stamped with a cross of the Order of Christ on one side and with a sphere—the device of the King D. Manuel—on the other; that the silver coin was equivalent in weight to a *bargani*, which coin was called *espera, i.e.*, esfera or sphere; that therew as also a *mea-espera*, or a 'half-sphere,' and lastly there were copper moneys called *leaes*, and other smaller copper pieces called *dinheiros*, three of which went to the *leal*. According to this authority, the gold coins, here called *cruzados*, were equal to seventeen *barganis*, but their value was raised in order to prevent their being taken away out of the country. This may be tabulated thus:—

COPPER.

Dinheiro		the smallest copper coin.
3 Dinheiros	=	one leal.

SILVER.

Meia (or half) espera	=	one vintem or 20 reis.
One espera...........	=	40 reis, which were again equal to one bargani.

GOLD.

Cruzado	=	680 reis, or seventeen barganis.

A somewhat different version is given of this coinage by Gaspar Correa in his *Lendas*, Cap. XI., Liv. II., p. 76. He tells us that the coins current in Goa at the time of the arrival of the Portuguese there were the gold *pardao, i. e.*, pagode or hûn, of the value of 360 reis, the silver *bargani* of 40 reis, and the copper *bazarucco* of 2 reis. D'Albuquerque's monetary system being analogous in size and value to the native one, although dissimilar in type, the object of the conqueror being, as above remarked, to displace the former currency by his own, he caused to be issued the gold cruzado of 420 reis, the silver bargani of 2 vintens, and the copper leal of the weight of a bazarucco, each leal being again sub-divided into four smallest copper pieces called cepayqua. This *statement* reduced to a table runs thus :—

COPPER.

Cepayqua, the smallest copper coin, of the value of half a real, and of the weight of 115 grains. Four *cepayquas* were equal to one *leal,* or one bazarucco of 2 reis of 460 grains.

SILVER.

10 leaes, or meia espera	=	20 reis of 40 grains.
20 leaes, or uma espera	=	40 reis of 80 grains.

GOLD.

10½ esperas, or um cruzado or manuel = 420 reis of 65 grains.[2]

The excess of 60 reis in a cruzado over the value of a pagoda is ascribed to the object D'Albuquerque had in view of raising the value of his gold to prevent its exportation. It was eventually raised to 480 reis.

The annalists are silent upon the existence of a meio manuel in gold, although a specimen of this coin is described by Mr. Lopes Fernandes in his *Memoria das Moedas correntes em Portugal.*[3] Its weight is 32½ grains, 22 carats fine.

Obv.—MEA. Above it a crown and a point.

Rev.—A sphere. Circular area, *grènetis,* or dotted rim. (See Plate II., fig. 1.)

Both the silver and copper coins bore on the obverse the letter A, probably the initial of Asia, and on the reverse the sphere.

The fineness of the gold and silver coins is said to have been of the highest degree.

As regards the word MEA, some writers, such as Severino de Faria, in his *Noticias de Portugal,* believe it to be the Latin for 'mine,' intended to show that the sphere given to D. Manuel for a device by King John II. had been deserved by the former, through the glorious acquisition during his reign of lands in India and Brazil to the Portuguese Crown; while others are of opinion that it stands for the Portuguese *meia,* or 'half,' the coin being a half-cruzado or manuel.

---

[2] The weight has been fixed by referring the value of these coins to that of the coins current in Portugal in the reign of the King D. Manuel.

[3] Vol. I., p. 121, Lisbon, 1856.

LÂMINA II

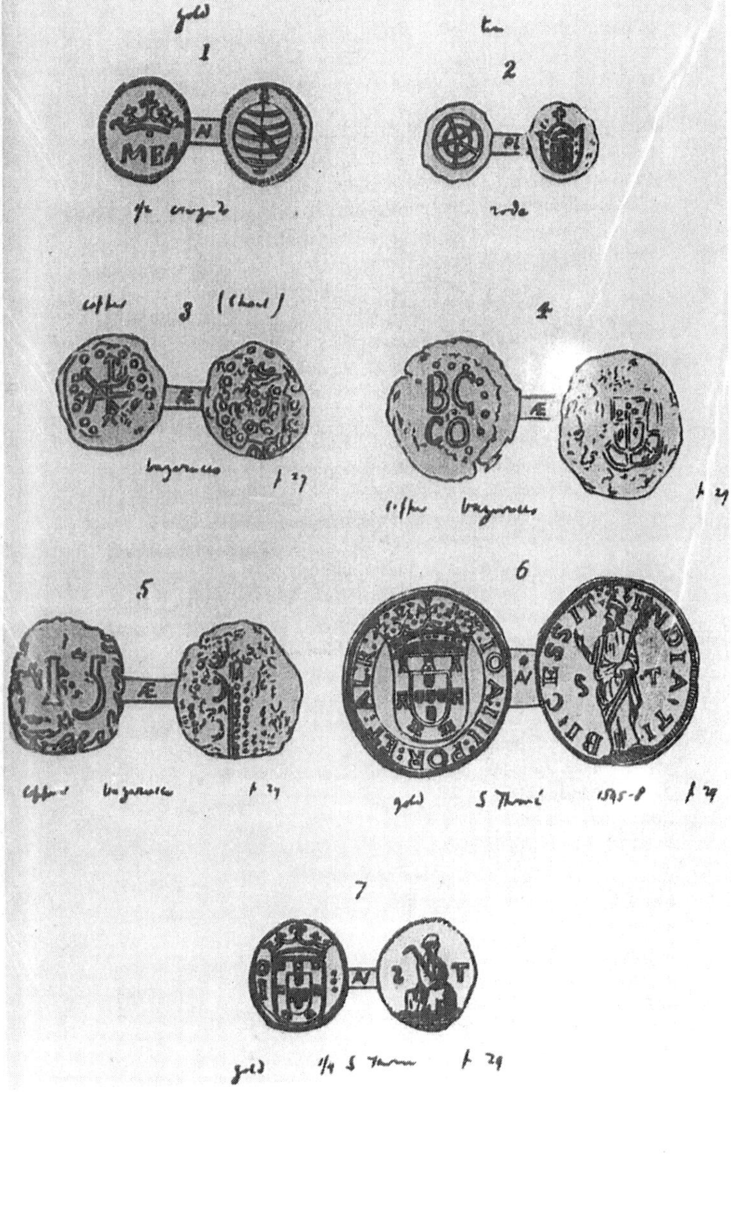

Two points of considerable interest in the numismatic history of this, as of the succeeding periods, are the relative values of gold and silver, and the metrical division of money. Leaving out of account copper, which has always been less liable to fluctuation, we learn that at the time of the Pathán rule the relative value of gold and silver was 8 : 1. In later times of the same dynasty the ratio was raised to 10 : 1, and in the reign of Akbár it remained the same. Between these two periods D'Albuquerque's system was brought in vogue, which, according to Gaspar Correa, maintains the proportion of 10 : 1, the ⅓ above 10 being the excess established on the ground of preventing its exportation. When later on the value of the cruzado was raised to 480 reis, the ratio became 12 : 1.

As regards metrology, D'Albuquerque's system appears to have been a mixture of the decimal and duodecimal division of money. Although the quartenary scale has always prevailed in India, and is indeed "the heritage of the masses" in this as in other countries, still decimal division has often been enforced by law. But in spite of this, and of men of science and legislators recommending the adoption of the latter, on account of the greater practical facility in arithmetical operations and accounts to be performed with numerals, people still persist in thinking duodecimally, even when obliged by law to express themselves decimally. The reason of this is believed to be the value of the products of nature and of human industry being regulated by the time and labour involved in them. Now these two elements, especially the time,—which is in reality the usual measure of labour, its exchangeable value being well expressed in the English proverb "time is money,"—is divided by nature duodecimally. The four seasons, the twelve months, the four weeks, the twenty-four hours, the twelve signs of the Zodiac, and so on, are all duodecimally divided. This natural arrangement is not less exemplified by our rupees, annas, and pies, than by the regulations contained in the *Ain-i-Akbári* of Abúl-Fazl and by the ordinances of the old Code of Manu. We do not exactly know, then, what must have induced the eminent statesman to mix the two modes of reckoning, and thus to produce a hybrid monetary system.

The conquest of Goa took place on the 25th November 1510, and was followed the next year by that of Malacca, where D'Albuquerque established another mint, and coins in gold, silver, and tin were directed to be struck. The gold coin was called *catholico,* of the weight of a quarter of *tundia,* a native weight, and of the value of 1,000 reis. The silver coin was called *malaquete,* weighing also a quarter of *tundia,* and meant to set aside the Malacca coinage of equal weight and value. The tin coins were of three kinds, viz., the *dinheiro,* equivalent to the native coin of the same material called by the Portuguese 2 *caixas,* ten *dinheiros* called *soldo,* and ten *soldos* called *bastardo.* This looks something like a decimal scale.

Now about this time a tin coin called *roda* was uttered by the Senate or Municipality of Goa. In the First Part of this series I have already described the tutenag coins, which were the successors of the tin coinage. The *roda,* which had stamped on the obverse a wheel, representative of St. Catherine's wheel, the patron saint of Goa, and the coat-of-arms of the kingdom on the reverse (see Plate II., fig. 2) was the lowest coin. Its almost insignificant value gave rise to the proverb still current in Portuguese India "isso não vale uma roda," "that is not worth a *roda,*" although the coin has since a long time disappeared from circulation. The *roda,* again, is the only Christian coin which bears some resemblance to the Buddhist *chakra* or 'wheel,' the most prevalent symbol occurring on the numismatic and other monuments of that once widely-spread religion. It was either in the form of a disc surrounded by rays, the rays sometimes resembling an umbrella; others a loop containing the crescent-shaped termination of a *chaitya,* or in that of a disc joined with the sánkha-shell, which is now sacred to Vishnu.

The above-mentioned facts lead to two important results, viz., that tin was first used in comparatively recent times for currency purposes by the native princes at Malacca, from whence it was introduced by the Portuguese into Goa and other settlements; and that the word *cash* found stamped on the Madras copper coinage of the East India Company, with a Roman numeral attached to it to denote its value, may perhaps be traced to the *caixa* of the Portuguese, just as pagoda has been to *pagode.* Tin is indigenous to the Indian Archipelago. It is found in the island of Banca, in the Malayan Peninsula, and the islets on its coasts, from whence it is carried to China and other countries. J. Crawfurd[a] tells us that in the countries which produce tin, this metal seems naturally enough to have had recourse to as coin, and that tin coins called *pichis* form the small currency of several States in the Indian Archipelago, 5,600 *pichis* being equal to one Spanish dollar. Tin, lead, or tutenag coins appear to have been current from time immemorial. M. Lenormant[b]

[a] *Hist. of Ind. Arch.* : Edin., 1820, vol. I., p. 280.

[b] *La Monnaie dans l'Antiquité.* Paris, 1878, Tome I., pp. 207 *et seq.*

tells us that lead coins were current in Egypt and in France during the first and second centuries of our era under the Roman emperors and the kings of Numidia. Of tin pieces he mentions those of the King Dionysius of Syracuse and of the Roman Emperors Septimius Severus and Caracalla, in their province of Gallia, especially Brittany, the country of tin *par excellence*, and where Severus had undertaken an expedition. Lead or tutenag coins were also minted by the Andhra-bhṛitya kings of Southern India during the second century A.D.,[6] where they were also current under the princes of the Chalukya dynasty from the 6th to the 9th century.[7] Thus it seems that these metals were used for currency at an archaic period, and there is no evidence of their being employed at later times, such as at the advent of the Portuguese to the East, except at Malacca, from whence the fashion must have been imported into Goa and other Portuguese mint cities, such as Diu, Damaun, Bassein, and Chaul. Tin coin was current in Portuguese districts round about Bombay, and the English of Bombay issued—it may be for the sake of uniformity—theirs of the same material. The specimens of the latter coinage which have hitherto reached us appear to have been struck between 1708 and 1773, subsequent to the mutiny of the Bombay troops under Keigwin, the fusion of the old and new East India Companies into the United East India Company, and the creation of the three Presidencies ruled by Governors in Council, those of Calcutta, Madras, and Bombay, each of them absolute within its own limits, until the appointment of a Governor-General for all India in 1773. It is true that, during the time of the Commonwealth, pewter was employed in coining farthings, and some *pattern* farthings of tin were also prepared in the reign of Charles I. and the early part of that of Charles II., which were made current in 1684, and continued to be coined until 1692, when this currency ceased.[8] These dates are, however, too early to account for the existence of the Bombay tin coinage, which appears to be an imitation, from reasons to be mentioned hereafter, of a similar Portuguese mintage.

With regard to the word *caixa*, the *caches* of the French, and the *cash* of the English, such as one finds on the Madras paisâ, coined in England in 1803, bearing on the obverse the East India Company's arms and on the reverse the legend 'XX Cash' and the Persian بیست کلس چہار:

[6] *Jour B. B. R. As. Soc.*, 1877, pp. 303 *et seq.*

[7] *Madras Jour. of Lit. Soc.*, N. S., vols. III. and IV., pp. 220 *et seq*; and 75 *et seq* respectively.

[8] *Numismatic Chronicle*, 1877, pp. 358 *et seq*, and 1878, p. 304.

فلوس است (*Bíst kás chahár falús ast*), or 'Twenty *kas* make four *fals*,' its origin may perhaps be traced to the Sanskrit name of the metal itself; for it is not rare in the history of numismatology to meet with the designation of a coin by that of the metal it is made of, as in the instance of the *aureus*, a gold coin, introduced by the Romans into the Spanish peninsula, and current as late as the first two or three reigns of the Portuguese monarchy. The Sanskrit word above referred to for tin is कस्तीर (Kastîra), from which is supposed to be derived the Greek *κασσίτερος*, a word used by Homer, hence the name of *Cassiterides insulæ*, literally, 'the tin islands' applied to the Scilly Islands near England, and the Arabic *kasdir*, referred to by Prof. Rehatsek in his remarks on the present paper, and which latter word is said to have been imported by the Phœnicians from the East, possibly from Malacca, into western countries. The first syllable of *kastîra* may then have given origin to the *caixa* of the Portuguese. It must not be forgotten, however, that the Persian *kas* is also derived from the Sanskrit कर्ष (*karsha*), an ancient Indian weight, also called *karshapana*, being in Tamil corrupted into *kasu*, Toda *kas*, Chinese *cash*, and Ceylonese *kahapana*. The last term is also found in western cave inscriptions, having its exact counterpart in the *ket* of the Egyptian metrology.

At a somewhat later period the Portuguese in India issued *rodas* and their multiples of both tin and tutenag. This alloy, which has from time immemorial been used by the Chinese in the manufacture of the *gong*, is whitish in appearance, sonorous when struck, tough, strong, malleable, easily cast, hammered, and polished, and does not readily tarnish. With these attributes, this amalgam recommended itself to the mint-masters to the extent of superseding latterly the tin coinage altogether. When analysed, it yields of copper 40·4, zinc 25·4, nickel 31·6, and iron 2·6. Its name is believed to have been given to it first by the Portuguese in India, who must have got it from the Malayalam language, in which *tuṭṭu* is the name of a tutenag coin equal to 20 cash, or ¼ pice; if it is not derived from the English tutty, *tutia* in low Latin, *tuzia* in Italian, and *tuthie* in French for a sublimate of zinc or calamine collected in the furnace. The word for tin used by the Portuguese in India is *calaim*, while in Portugal it is called *estanho*. *Calaim* is evidently derived from the Indian vernaculars, for it is कल्हई (*kalhaî*) in Marâṭhî, કલઈ (*kalai*) in Gujarathi, and قلعی (*kalai*) in Hindustani.

But to return to the imitation tin coinage of Bombay. It was not only by the adoption of this material for their coinage, but even by the imitation of types and symbols, which were originally Portuguese, that the rising power of the English of Bombay gave a tacit proof of their appreciation of the inventive power of their allies and neighbours, the Portuguese, whose star was now declining, but were still masters of all the districts round about Bombay up to the year 1740. The Portuguese of Chaul had struck a copper *bazarucco*, bearing a sheaf of arrows and a bow on the obverse, and the coat-of-arms of the kingdom on the reverse (see Plate II., fig. 3). This coin was issued some time prior to 1577, and must have been current in the environs of Bombay. This device is found engraven on one of the ruined gates of that once famous city. The gate was built in 1577, as testified to by an inscription, a facsimile of which, with a lithograph representing the gate itself, are inserted in my work on that city.* The gate is surmounted by the well-known D. Manuel's terrestrial globe, three arrows in a sheaf, the coat-of-arms of the kingdom of Portugal, and the cross of the Order of Christ above them all. Here the globe denotes the power, the broad belt which encircles it being intended to represent the conquests and discoveries of the Portuguese throughout the world, and the three arrows tied together peace, which the Portuguese of Chaul had enjoyed, before the building of this part of the fortifications, uninterruptedly for thirty long years, which was an unusual occurrence in those troublous times.

Now the three arrows tied together were engraven or represented not only on lithic, but even on numismatic monuments of the Portuguese in India. The English of Bombay copied this emblem on their copper pieces, bearing on one side a crown and on the other three arrows tied together, flanked by the letters *G.* and *R.* in italic for Georgius and Rex, with the legend *Auspicio Regis et Senatus Angliæ* below. To the Portuguese, who appear to have imitated this device from a Spanish coin current in Portugal between 1557 and 1641, called *real de prata*, or 'silver real,' it was an emblem of peace, to the English of Bombay probably a mere ornament, if not a meaningless type.

II.

D'Albuquerque died on the 16th December 1515, at the age of 63, after serving ten years in the East, and was succeeded by Lopes Soares de Albergaria. His coinage supplied the monetary need of Portuguese India to the extent of his successors for some years minting only copper

* *History and Antiquities of Chaul and Bassein*: Bombay, 1876, p. 81.

money. Two important documents give us a glimpse of the operations carried on in the Goa mint about this time. Fernão D'Alcaçova, *Vedor da Fazenda*, or Superintendent of His M.'s Treasury, in his *Regimento*, or 'Mint Regulation,' says that to mint one *quintal* of copper (a Portuguese weight equal to 129 lbs. 5 oz. and 5 drs.) in 1517, it cost 1,042 reis, yielding 3,744 *leaes*, equivalent to 23¼ pardaos, or 18 cruzados and 288 reis, each pardao at the rate of 320 reis. Then, of each *quintal* five parts were coined into *leaes*, and one into *pequeninos, i.e.*, cepayquas.[10] On the 13th November 1518 the Governor Diogo Lopes de Siqueira, who governed India from 1518 to 1522, published a proclamation allowing people to carry away out of the country all sorts of coins, that is, copper and tin pieces, except gold and silver ones.[11] And, in a legislative enactment dated the 23rd March 1519, the same Governor allows the Portuguese coinage to leave the country, especially the copper money, hoping thereby to increase its circulation, but forbids the minting of more silver or gold coins. This was probably the result of having an abundance of the latter coinage on account of its value having been raised to prevent exportation.

Then follows a long interval of time, during which no change appears to have been made in the above-mentioned mint regulations. In the mean time King D. Manuel died in 1521, being succeeded by D. João III.

During the governorship of Nuno da Cunha, from 1529 to 1538, copper money was ordered to be coined, the cost of the metal being 16 pardaos per one quintal, which indicates a considerable fall in the value of copper from the time of the two immediate successors of D'Albuquerque. D. Garcia de Noronha, who ruled between 1538 and 1540, also directed the issue of copper pieces, the document noticing this fact stating that the price of copper was now rising, being 18 pardaos per one quintal.

In the year 1542, the first of the Governor Martim Affonso de Souza's rule, which ended in 1545, the denomination of copper pieces was changed from *leaes* into bazaruccos. The value of copper was raised to 36 pardaos per one quintal, which is said to have given rise to discontent among the people, as the market value of the metal was only 18 to 20 pardaos a quintal. Of bazaruccos there were three different types, first the one bearing on the obverse a sheaf of arrows above de-

[10] *Archivo Portuguez Oriental*, Fasciculo V., Pt. I. : Goa, 1865, pp. 8-9.

[11] *Archivo ut supra*, p. 31. *Opus. cit.*, p. 10. *Opus. cit.* : Fasc. I., p. 25, and Fasc. II., p. 174.

scribed and struck at Chaul; the second the letters BCCO on one side, and the royal coat-of-arms on the other; and the third a number, such as 15, with a star above and below, to indicate its value on the obverse, and CCC to the left, and dotted area to the right, on the reverse. (See Plate II., figs. 4 and 5.) All these bazaruccos have some dots round the area, which may be intended to mark the number of bazaruccos, not unlike the dots on the silver coins of King D. Affonso VI. of Portugal, each dot standing for one hundred reis, and those on the sub-division of the Roman *as*, the *uncia* having one, the *sextans* two, the *quadrans* three, and the *triens* four, or a partially obliterated dotted rim.

The Viceroy D. João de Castro, whose rule extended from 1545 to 1548, directed the issue of copper bazaruccos alone, with the advice of the Bishop of the Diocese, D. João de Albuquerque, at the rate of 25 pardaos the quintal, that being near the market price. D. João de Castro's successor, Garcia de Sá, who governed from 1548 to 1549, introduced during the brief tenure of his office an innovation into the monetary system, which had a lasting effect, and made his name, next to that of D'Albuquerque, the most memorable in the Indo-Portuguese annals of currencies. He directed the issue of a gold coin called S. Thomé, or 'St. Thomas,' 20½ carats fine, weight 193¼ grains, and value 1,000 reis. (See Plate II., fig. 6.)

Obv.—IOA III., POR. ET. AL. R. The coat-of-arms of the kingdom in the centre of the area.

Rev.—INDIA TIBI CESSIT. The figure of St. Thomas, standing, head to the right, letters S and T on each side of the saint. Dotted rims. Very rare.

A quarter of the above coin was also struck; weight 48 grains. Also very rare.

Obv.—The coat-of-arms of the kingdom in the middle, and İ. on the left and ⁝ on the right.

Rev.—The figure of St. Thomas, seated, to the right holding a club on the right shoulder, and the letters S and T on the sides. (See Plate II., fig. 7.)

The İ. on the left side of the coat-of-arms stands for IOÄO, and the three points on the right for III., *i.e.*, King John III. Some authors call the first coin Double St. Thomas, and the second, Half St. Thomas, and the weight of the latter shows it to be a quarter of the former. Diogo do Couto, in his *Decadas*, says of this coin:—" Feeling the want of money in the city, the Governor commanded the issue of a gold coin of the fineness of the *round pagodes*, which are brought from the mainland, of 43 points, equal to 20¼ (carats), each mark of gold yielding 67 coins of 2 *tangas*, 8 grains, and 16 parts of a grain. He directed to strike this coin, stamping on one side the figure of the blessed Apostle St. Thomas, the Patron Saint of India, and the *quinas* or the royal coat-of-arms of Portugal on the other. This coin was called *S. Thomé*, which is current now throughout India. Private individuals coining gold money in the Royal Mint had to pay for each mark of the bullion coined two St. Thomés, one to the King, and one to the officers of the mint." *Dec.* VI., Liv. 7, Cap. I. Diogo do Couto began to write his history in 1597, in continuation of the *Decadas* of João de Barros. With regard to the words *pagodes redondos* or 'round pagodas,' which are elsewhere called *pardaos redondos*, and *tanga*, I reserve my remarks for the Third Part of this series.

The Viceroy Affonso de Noronha, who governed India from 1550 to 1554, ordered the coining of S. Thomé of silver, sometimes called *patacões*. This was the first silver coinage by the successors of D'Albuquerque, for from 1510 to 1550 no silver coin was minted; except the *esperas*, struck during the first days of the conquest of Goa. All these forty years the silver coins were supplied from the neighbouring countries, as well as the gold coinage.[12] The *patacões* directed to be minted by the Viceroy Affonso de Noronha were of the fineness of 11 *dinheiros*, this fineness representing 11 of silver and 1 of copper, or 916⅔ of silver and 83⅓ of copper in 1,000. One mark of silver yielded 8 *patacões* and 4 tangas, which was eventually raised to 8⅛ patacões, and at last to 9½, which is said to have been done to the prejudice of the Royal Treasury.[13] In the year 1554 Antonio Nunes, who was about this time *tanadar* or *almoxarife* (receiver of customs, superintendent of royal demesnes) at Agassi, in the settlement of Bassein, wrote his *Livro dos Pezos, Medidas, e Moedas*, or "Book of Weights, Measures, and Coins," published as late as 1858, under the Royal Academy of Sciences of Lisbon, which is an important document, considering the time when it was written, and the amount of information it contains. He gives a long table of the coins current in the Portuguese settlements in the East, as well as in the neighbouring States, telling at the same time

---

[12] *Arch. Port. Orient.*, Fasc. II., p. 175.

[13] *Ibid.*

their value in Portuguese reis. I append below a few extracts, essential for the due elucidation of the subject, in alphabetical order :—

Coins current in Bassein in 1554.

Fedea (a nominal coin)	=	15 reis.
Pardao, equal to 5 tangas in silver	=	300 ,,
Tanga in silver, equal to 4 fedeas.	=	60 ,,

BENGAL.

Larim	=	48 pones or 60 reis.
Pone	=	80 cauris.

Cauri is the shell imported into India from the Maldive Islands, known to the naturalists as *cypræa moneta*, and sometimes called by the Portuguese *buzio*.

Caile, Calicut, Chale, Cananor, Ceylon, Coulão, Negapatão, and Paleacote—

Fanam of base gold, also called chacram	=	25 reis (variable).
Raja of base gold, current in Coulão	=	40 ,,
Portuguez in gold, current in Ceylon, worth 15 xerafins ...	=	4,500 ,,

Fanão or fanam varied in value from 10 reis in Ceylon to 29 in Negapatão. In Paleacote 10 fanams made the *pardao de fanões*.

COCHIN.

Pardao of gold	=	360 reis.
Xerafim........................	=	300 ,,
Fanam	=	$21\frac{2}{3}$,,
Cruzado of gold	=	390 ,,

The value of this cruzado rose from 390 reis to 426 in the governorship of Martim Affonso de Souza. In the purchase of pepper, 19 fanams made one cruzado in gold.

DIU.

Axiry (silver coin), worth 60 fedeas, or 11 perogis	=	111 reis.
Pardao of $42\frac{1}{2}$ perogis	=	360 ,,

Fedea was a nominal coin of the value of nearly 2 reis, and a perogi was equal to 8 reis.

GOA.

Tanga of 50 leaes	=	60 reis.	
Pardao of 5 tangas	=	300 ,,	
Pardao in gold of 6 tangas. .	=	360 ,,	(liable to fluctuate).
Leal............................	=	$1\frac{1}{5}$,,	
Tanga in silver	=	72 ,,	(liable to fluctuate about 8 or 10 per cent.)
Tanga branca of 4 barganis.	=	$115\frac{1}{5}$,,	
Bargani of 24 leaes	=	$28\frac{4}{5}$,,	
Vintem of 15 leaes	=	18 ,,	

Besides the above, there were current at Goa the Venetian sequin, the sultani, abraemo, and cruzado in gold, as well as the xerafim of Aden and Ormuz—the former four worth 7 tangas, or 420 reis ; the latter two 360 and 300 reis, respectively. The same coins were current also at Chaul and at Batecalá, with the addition of the copper bazarucco in use in Chaul of the value of 3 reis each. The madrafaxão of Cambay was equal to 1,440 reis, variable.

ORMUZ.

Faluz of 10 dinars	=	$1\frac{1}{5}$	reis (nearly).	
Cadi of 100 dinars	=	13	,,	,,
Azar of 10 cadis	=	140	,,	,,
Pardao of 2 azares...............	=	280	,,	,,
Xerafim in gold	=	300	,,	
Tanga in silver, also called larim.	=	62	,,	(liable to fluctuate as far as 70 reis).[14]

But to return to the chronological series. Between the years 1554 and 1555, during which time D. Pedro Mascarenhas was Viceroy, the silver *patacões* were continued to be coined, raising at the same time the price of a mark of silver to 3,540 reis. His successor, Francisco Barretto, who ruled from 1555 to 1558, made no change in the issue of this coin, which he kept on minting at the same rate of value, the 3,540 reis per one mark being divided into 3,300 for the owner of the bullion and 240 for signorage, expenses of mintage, and so on. The unwarrantable elevation in the price of silver gave rise to some conten-

[14] *Subsidios para a Historia da India Portugueza*, by R. J. de L. Felner: Lisbon, 1868, Pt. I., pp. 61 *et seq.*

tion. This elevation seems to have resulted from the Government allowing private individuals to issue coins, when the latter not only raised the price of silver, but even deteriorated the assay fineness of the coin. In Rome, under the Republic, a similar state of things appears to have existed, and was eventually put a stop to, as prejudicial to the interests of the State. Though the State held the management of the mint, any family or *gens* or private individual was entitled to coin money at the public expense, deriving of course some profit to himself. This system was, nearly eighteen centuries after, found as obnoxious at Goa as it was in Rome.

We have now arrived at an epoch of considerable historical importance, a period of transition, the turning-point, so to speak, in the fortune of the Portuguese in the East. In 1557 King D. João III. died, and was succeeded by his grandson D. Sebastião. The first Viceroy of King D. Sebastião was Constantino de Bragança, who ruled India from 1558 to 1561. Although his name is famous in the conquest of Damaun and in the destruction of the *dalada*, or tooth relic of Gautama Buddha, said to be in Ceylon still, in the history of numismatics he is the least conspicuous of all the Viceroys of India. The only thing he did, was to direct the issue of copper money at the rate of 42 xerafims the quintal, when the market value of copper was only 25 pardaos. He was succeeded by Conde de Redondo, who governed from 1561 to 1564. He commanded the coining of copper bazaruccos at the rate of 35 pardaos of tangas the quintal of copper, including all expenses. His successor, D. Antão de Noronha, who ruled between 1564 and 1568, issued a proclamation forbidding the coining of silver S. Thomés, or patacões, as prejudicial both to the State and people, directing those extant to circulate for their silver value. The cause of this prohibition will be explained in Part III.

Between the years 1568 and 1571 the Viceroy D. Luis d'Athaide held the helm of government, and has an important place in the numismatic history of Portuguese India. It was he who gave the first Code of Regulations for the mint, and commanded to continue the issue of gold S. Thomés of 43 points, or $20\frac{1}{4}$ *quilates*, each mark of gold yielding 67 S. Thomés and two tangas, and each S. Thomé weighing 68 grains and 16 parts of a grain. A Portuguese mark of gold is equal to $3,542\frac{2}{5}$ English grains. The fineness of gold is expressed in *quilates* or carats, the mark fine being 24 carats. *Carante* is also an old Portuguese expression for carat.

This Viceroy also directed to utter silver coins known as *bastião*, the double *bastião*, and the half, and silver tangas. The value of the first was 300 reis, 600 of the second, and 150 of the third. His silver was 11 dinheiros fine, the mark fine being 12 dinheiros. None of these coins are extant, nor have we any examples of the coinage of the six of his predecessors. His bastião had the figure of St. Sebastian, in honour of the king of this name, on one side, and the royal coat-of-arms on the other; while his silver tangas had an arrow on the obverse, probably a symbol of the martyrdom of the saint, and the same coat-of-arms on the reverse. The same Viceroy, by his order dated the 16th November 1568, commanded the issue of gold and silver coinage by the Cochin mint.[15]

His successors in the viceroyalty, D. Antonio de Noronha, Antonio Moniz Barretto, and D. Diogo de Menezes, between 1571 and 1578, made no alteration in the coinage, nor do they appear to have directed the continuation of the former issues until D. Luis de Athaide came out to India a second time as Viceroy, honoured with the title of Conde de Attoguia, on the 31st August 1578, and died in Goa on the 10th March 1581. The currency ordered by his proclamation, dated the 27th August 1569, to be referred to hereafter, continued to prevail during his absence from India, and now he commanded the coining of xerafims of 5 tangas of the assay fineness of one larim of copper in two larims and a half of silver.

In the mean time King D. Sebastião disappeared, was most probably slain in his African expedition, and Cardinal D. Henrique mounted the throne of Portugal. On his death in 1580, Philip II. of Spain was crowned at Lisbon.

We have thus arrived at the end of the first period of our Numismatic History of Portuguese India. Two other papers will conclude the series, filling up exactly the space of three centuries, each paper describing the numismatic period of 150 years, viz., the first from the union of Portugal with Spain in 1580 until 1730, and the second from that date to the present year 1880.

---

[15] *Arch. Port. Orient.*, Fasc. V., Pt. II., p. 692.

LAMINA III

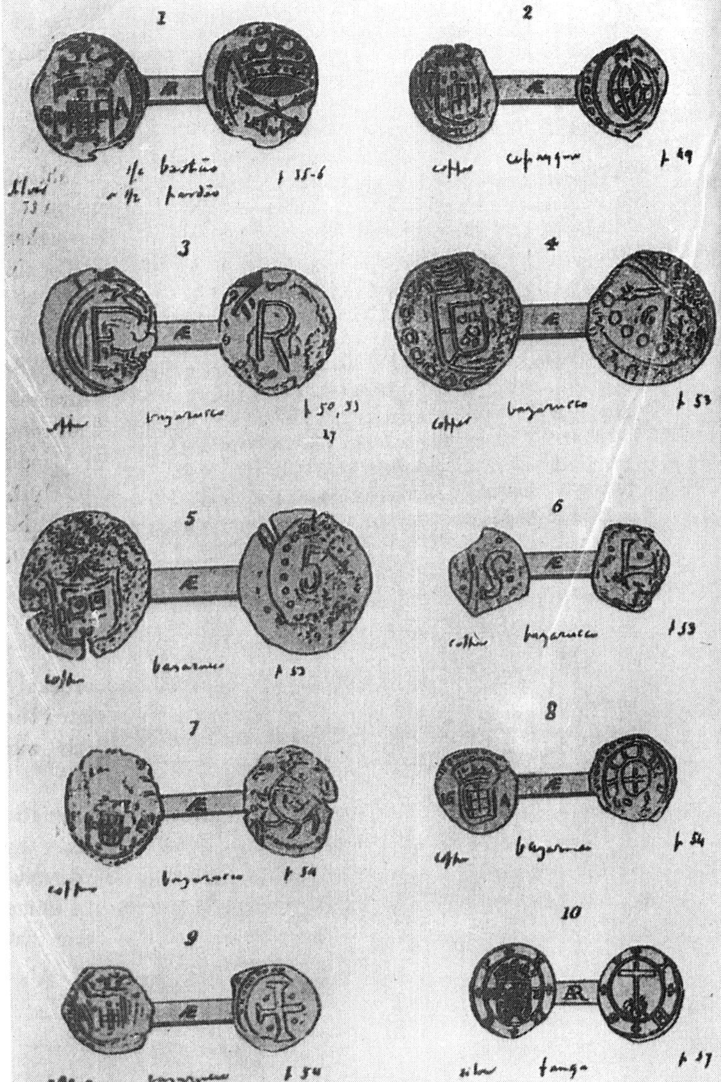

CONTRIBUTIONS

TO THE

STUDY OF INDO-PORTUGUESE NUMISMATICS.

BY

J. GERSON DA CUNHA,

M.R.C.S. AND L.M., ENG.; L.R.C.P., EDIN.;

Knight of the Order of St. Gregory the Great; Member of the Committee of Management of the Bombay Branch of the Royal Asiatic Society; Member of the Royal Asiatic Society of Great Britain and Ireland; Corresponding Member of the Royal Academy of Sciences of Lisbon; of the Oriental Academy of Florence; of the Academy of Science, Literature and Arts of Lyon; of the Arcadia of Rome; of the Adriatic Society of the Natural Sciences of Trieste; of the I.R. Zoological and Botanical Society of Vienna; Fellow of the Geographical Society of Italy, and of that of Lisbon; Fellow of the University of Bombay, &c.

FASCICULUS III.

Bombay:

PRINTED AT THE

EDUCATION SOCIETY'S PRESS, BYCULLA.

1880.

FASCICULUS III.

I.

Following in chronological sequence the vicissitudes of the numismatic history of Portuguese India, I must begin with the year 1580, when the sovereignty of Portugal passed from Cardinal D. Henrique to D. Filippe II. of Spain, the Viceroy of India being D. Luiz de Athayde, Conde de Athouguia, who came out a second time, and continued in office from 1578 to the 9th March 1581. During his first viceroyalty, from the 10th of September 1568 to the 6th of the same month in 1571, he issued, amongst other useful measures, important resolutions relating to the Portuguese coinage in India. By a provision dated the 15th of November 1568, he commanded the issue of gold and silver coinage at Cochin, of which no specimen has unfortunately been preserved. The minting of this money was however met with considerable opposition from the people, the causes of which will hereafter be inquired into, when the viceroy gave a new regulation to the Mint on the 27th of August 1569. This new code of rules for the minting of money at Goa established that the future issue of the gold coinage should be entitled S. Thomés, each piece weighing 68·8 Portuguese grains, of the fineness of 43 points, or 20¼ carats, while the silver currency was to consist of *bastiões*, in substitution for the debased *patacões*, with its divisions of *meio bastião, tanga*, &c.

The coins extant of this coinage are the following:—

I. *Obverse*—P. R. (*Portugaliæ Rex*), the effigy of S. Sebastian standing to the right, pierced by four arrows. Round the margin a dotted rim, or *grènetis*.

Reverse—The coat-of-arms of the kingdom; on the left G and on the right A, the initial and final letters of Goa.

II. *Obverse*—Two arrows placed crosswise in the field, tied together in the form of the letter X, surmounted by a royal crown.

Reverse—The arms of the kingdom, having on the sides the letters G and A. The dotted rim, as in No. I. (See Plate III., fig. 1.)

All the coins are represented of the exact size.

Both the above coins are described by Mr. Teixeira de Aragão in his *Descripção Geral e Historica das Moedas Cunhadas em nome dos Reis, &c.*, Tome III., Lisbon, 1880, p. 154, and illustrated at Pl. I., figs. 10 and 11. Both coins are of silver. The weight of the first is given by the above-cited writer as 381 Portuguese grains, and the coin is said to be preserved in the collection of the late F. N. Xavier of Goa, while that of the second is 184 Portuguese grains. They are, moreover, called *bastião* or *pardao* and *meio bastião* or *meio pardao*, respectively. An example of the latter piece is also in the collection of Mr. J. M. de Sousa e Brito of Goa, who kindly lent it for illustrating this paper. Its weight is 147 grains troy. It is however supposed by some *connoisseurs* that this coin was struck during the reign of Cardinal Henrique.

The code of regulations given to the Mint of Goa by D. Luiz de Athayde in 1569 was put into execution not only during the first term of his viceroyalty, which ended in 1571, but also in the subsequent period filled up by the viceroys D. Antonio de Noronha, Antonio Moniz Barreto and D. Diogo de Menezes, who did nothing more than sign some provisions relative to the copper coinage, called *bazaruccos*, to be referred to further on, and to some other insignificant monetary matters. On his return to India in 1578, D. Luiz found his mint regulations in full force, which he completed by adding to the former issues of money that of a coin called *xerafim*, of the value of five *tangas*, of an alloy of silver and copper, in the proportion of one *larin* of copper to two and a half *larins* of silver.

Before proceeding on with the record of successive coinages struck under the rule of each viceroy in consecutive order, it may not perhaps be inopportune to consider here, for the clearer elucidation of the subject, the origin and meanings of each of these terms—viz., xerafim, tanga, and larim.

II.

The word "*xerafim*" is evidently derived from the Persian اشرفی (*ashrafī*), which was a gold coin, weighing about fifty grains, and being equal in this respect, if not in fineness, to the Venetian sequin or Dutch ducat.

Although originally Persian money, it became in course of time current in the Gulf of Cambay and in the countries along the Malabar Coast. The Portuguese were the first to adopt this designation for one of their coins, and the East India Company applied it also to the gold *muhr* (مهر *muhr*, 'a seal,') struck at Mûrshedabâd, to distinguish it from the *muhr* issued in 1819, in which the absolute quantity of pure metal was reduced by adding $\frac{1}{12}$th of alloy, in order to adjust the ratio of its value to that of silver, while the *ashrafî* always maintained a high degree of purity (99¾ touch), and weighed, by the regulations of May 1793, a little more than 190 grains troy.[1]

Filippo Sassetti, an Italian traveller of the sixteenth century, writing to his friend, AlessandroRinuccini, of Florence, about 1585, refers to these *xerafins*, struck at Goa, which he writes *xaraffi*, connecting the word with *ṣarraf*, 'a money-changer,' which he writes elsewhere *xaraffo*, and derives from the latter the term *xarafaggio*, which he defines as the rate of exchange. As the passage is an interesting one, and relates to the period under discussion, I shall quote it here:—"Ora, sì come costà tra noi," he writes, "sono qua i banchieri, e fra essi ha d' uomini molto ricchi, e altri che per mantenere il banco loro aperto non hanno se non tanti basalucchi quanti bastano a cambiare una moneta d' ora e d' argento, pigliandone l' aggio, d' onde si sostentano; ch' è ora più ora meno, secondo l'abbondanza dell' oro ò della moneta. Chiamansi questi banchieri *xaraffi*, servendo l' *x* alla spagnuola per *s*. Di qui potrete riconoscere questo nome, facendosi menzione no so se nel Boccaccio o nel Novellino di tanti saraffi che furono dati, credo da Saladino, a non so chi, che per questo nome veniva anticamente a chiamarsi la moneta,[2] sì come oggi si chiama ancora certa molto trista che battono qui i Portoghesi in Goa, detti *xarafini*, che la piglierebbero da' Gentili."[3]

The connection between *xerafins* and *shroffs*, *i. e.*, between *ashrafî* and *ṣarraf* is entirely an imaginary one; for while *ashrafî* is derived, as it seems, from the Arabic شريف (*sherif*) 'noble,' اشرف (*ashraf*) its comparative, gold being the noble metal *par excellence*, the word *shroff*, common enough in our Indian bazârs, is derived from the Persian صراف (*ṣarrāf*), a money-changer, exchanger, or 'cambist,' from صرف (*ṣarf*), 'changing,' 'turning,' &c.

---

[1] *Prinsep's Ind. Ant.* Lond. 1858. Vol. II., U. T., p. 5.

[2] To the above quotation my learned friend, Count De Gubernatis, of Florence, adds this footnote—Nulla di più servile che la moneta, la quale muta nome ad ogni mutar di padrone," which is true enough, but not in the case of our shroffs, who, instead of being masters, are servants of money.

[3] *Storia dei Viaggiatori Italiani nelle Indie Orientali.* By Angelo De Gubernatis. Livorno, 1875, p. 301.

Now with regard to the word *tanga*, this is, unlike the *xerafim*, derived from an Indian source. When the Portuguese conquered Goa, they found the revenue accounts computed, amongst other coins, by what the natives called *tanké*, with their divisions and sub-divisions of *barganis* and *zoitolés*.[4] It was but natural for the conqueror to adapt the old monetary nomenclature to the new currency, as he did, with some phonetic alterations. Thus he changed *tanké* into *tanga*, which was in those days divided into two kinds—viz., *tanga branca*, or 'white tanga,' which was but an imaginary coin, or money of account, not unlike the *mark* of the Anglo-Saxon kings, the *mancus*, *ora* or *thrimsa*, both of them being nominal sums rather than actual coins, and the *tanga* proper.

The *tanga branca* expressed a value equal to four *barganis*, which latter term was also of mere computation, introduced most probably by the Muhammadan predecessors of the Portuguese into Goa, and although variable, the average value could perhaps be fixed for all commercial purposes by taking one *barganim* as equal to twenty-four *leaes* or *bazaruccos*, while twenty-three *barganis* went to a pagoda of 360 reis.

These *bazaruccos* or *leaes* were copper coins struck by command of d'Albuquerque in 1510. They bore on the obverse a sphere, and on the reverse the royal coat-of-arms with A, the initial of Asia, or of Albuquerque, as others say.

Although the Portuguese borrowed the word from the natives of the country, which word was, moreover, used in the neighbouring principalities, being *tankam* where Telegu is spoken, and *taka* in the Dakhaṇ, to signify a copper coin equal to 16 *paisas* or *dabbs*, it seems still to be of a far remoter antiquity. We may, perhaps, trace the origin of this word to the Sanskṛit टङ्क (ṭank), its other form being टङ्ग (ṭaṅg), which approaches more closely the Portuguese *tanga*. Now *ṭank* or *ṭang*, in Sanskṛit, means not only a weight equal to four mashas, but also a stamped coin, specially of silver. Then we have the Sanskṛit compounds of *Ṭanka-śálá*, 'a mint,' and *Ṭanka-pati*, the master of the mint; while the old Tamil name for a mint is *kambattam*.[5] The Muhammadan rulers of India did eventually Persianize, so to speak, the word ṭank into تنکه (*tánke*), and this name *tânke* we find applied to coins struck from the time of Mahmud of Ghazni. There were both silver and copper *tánkes* then, just as the Portuguese had their silver

[4] *Memoria sobre as Moedas Cunhadas em Goa.* By F. N. Xavier. Nova-Goa, 1866, p. 55, *et seq.*

[5] *Madras Journal of Literature and Science.* 1858. Vol. XIX., p. 231.

and copper *tangas* some centuries after. But the *tánkes* of Sikandar Lodi were mere mixtures of both silver and copper, and from their extremely variable character were not used in revenue returns. Sikandar Lodi did perhaps in this respect more than pursue the monetary policy of Muhammad bin Tughlak, who deteriorated the currency, and resorted to the extreme measure of forced currency. He attempted to introduce brass medals instead of money, imitating the paper-currency of China, but after a futile trial, he aimed at restoration of the ancient purity of the metal. It was this debasement of his coin which gave rise to the denominations of *tanka núkra* and *tanka siáh, i. e.*, 'white or real tankah of silver,' and 'black tankah.' It appears that there were in the mediæval times, when the great unit was the *taka* of not less than 145 grains (*śataka* or *ser* being *śat-taka* or 100 takas), both gold and silver tankahs, the orthography of which has been preserved by Ibn Batuta as تنكه, while the weight of the copper tankah was a little higher. But Baber, in his memoirs, gives a tank as a weight equal to 58·95 grains, whereas the Delhi tankah contained absolutely 173 grains, and the theoretical issued weight of 175 grains, and a touch of nearly pure silver. There was then the *kani*, a fraction, a mere weight of the tankah, *i. e.*, $\frac{1}{64}$ of 175 grains, which is said to be of Drâviḍian source, and pronounced *canny*, but in the Koṅkaṇ the word *kono* is used for 'a grain,' while *do-kani*, or '2 kanis,' is a well-known copper coin. Lastly, there was a coin of half a tankah. The authorized tankah of the Pathán dynasty is by Arabs called *dinar* of silver. Such was the extremely inconvenient diversity in the name, value, and weight of a coin, which was a common currency of a considerable part of India in the middle ages. It was but natural for the Portuguese, under those circumstances, to adopt a name familiar to the people, but in the design they of course furnished their own prototypes. The Emperor Akbar appears to have been the first to fix a standard for this coin by means of his *yak tánke-i-Akbar Sháhi*, and, as we are informed by the *Aîn-i-Akbarî*, 5 tánkes made one *dám*, and 40 *dáms* one rupee. But before this time, the value of the *tanga*, from Ormuz in the Persian Gulf to Cambay and the Malabar Coast, was as variable as the weight *tola* (Sk. तोलक *tolaka*, Hind. تولا *tolá*,) in different parts of India, as witnessed by the Portuguese chroniclers of the period.[6]

Nikitin, who travelled in India in the 14th century, mentions tenka, described by his editor as *tankha*, represented by the rupee of Akbar,

[6] *Subsidios para a Historia da India Portugueza.* By R. J. de L. Felner. Lisbon, 1868. Pt. I., 25, 32; Pt. II., 20, 46; and Pt. III., 36, 51.

which remained unaltered from his time to the middle of the last century.[7]

Larim, described by Meninski as "larinus, monetæ Persicæ genus, ex argento," was a Persian silver coin, originally current on the coasts of the Persian Gulf, but the use of which was propagated, and its manufacture imitated, in India. Its name is derived from the place where the original Larim was struck—viz., Lar or Laristan, the capital city of Caramania Deserta, a petty principality, which was finally reduced by Shah Abbas the Great, and which, by its possession of Gombrun, the chief emporium on the Gulf, had commercial relations with Cambay, the Malabar Coast and Ceylon. Camões mentions this place in his poem thus:—

"Aqui de Dom Philippe de Menezes
Se mostrará a virtude em armas clara,
Quando com muito poucos Portuguezes
Os muitos Párseos vencerá de Lara:
Virão provar or golpes e revezes
De Dom Pedro de Souza, que provára
Ja seu braço em Ampaza, que deixada
Terá por terra á fôrça só de espada."

Canto x., estancia civ.[8]

---

[7] *Major's India in the 15th Century*. Lond. 1857, p. 20.

[8] *Obras de Luiz de Camões*. Lisboa. 1852. Tome I., p. 356.

With regard to the translation of the above stanza, although there are several translations of the *Lusiados* in English, I have not yet seen one to equal that of my friend, Captain Richard F. Burton, in the faithful rendering of the great Portuguese epic. His translation of the above passage runs thus:—

Here Dom Philippe do Menézes view
approved a doughty valiant man-at-arms,
who with his Portughueze exceeding few
shall quell the Lára Parsi's potent swarms:
Pedro de Souza too shall make them rue
reversèd Fortunes, Warfare's deadliest harms,
who had his prowess in Ampáza shown,
and took the land by sweep of sword alone."

Burton's Lusiads. Lond. 1881. Vol. II., p. 398.

Lara is a paragoge for Lar, which was well known to the Portuguese from its neighbourhood to their once rich settlement of Ormuz. But the early Portuguese authors write it Lara or Larah, and describe it as an island in the Persian Gulf. Pietro della Valle distinguished Lar from Larek, the former of which he describes as a city half way between Schiraz and Mina (*Viaggi.*, Pt. II. Venetia. 1667, p. 405), capital of a great province,

Lary or *Larym*, although the earliest description of the coin is ascribed by modern numismatists to Sir John Chirdin, the period of whose travels in Persia does not go before 1657, is mentioned by Felner, in a document dated 1525, describing it in the Index, thus:—"Larym, palavra que, só de per si, significa a tanga larym ou de Larah," while the document divides the coin into two kinds, old and new *larym*, the former being one dynar less than the latter. The coins of Lar are enumerated thus:—Two falus are equal to one dynar, twelve dynars equal to one tanga, and three tangas and ten dynars are equal to one new larym. But at somewhat later date the larym is generally called "tanga larym."

Chirdin describes it thus:—"Il y a une monnoye tout le long du Golphe Persique, nommée *Larins*, qui est celle dont on s'y sert le plus dans le commerce......Cette monnoye est d'argent fin et vaut deux *chayé* (shâhi) et demi, qui font onze sols trois deniers de notre monnoye. Elle est d'une figure tout extraordinaire, car c'est un fil rond, gros comme une plume à écrire, plié à deux, de la longueur d'un travers de pouce, avec une petite marque dessus qui est le coin du Prince......On dit qu'elle avoit cours autrefois dans tout l'Orient."[9] But about this time the coin had ceased to be current in Persia, or perhaps since the

---

owned formerly by a prince, who was dispossessed of it about twenty-three years before the visit of Della Valle, which took place in 1622, by Abbas, king of Persia (p. 433), and inhabited by learned men (p. 439). Larek he calls an island, in the middle of the Persian Gulf, not far from Ormuz. It is probably the Larah of the Portuguese. With regard to the city of Lar, a modern writer says:—"The town is estimated to contain 1,200 inhabited houses, and the people reckon ten souls to a house; but it is hard to believe, looking down on Lar from the limestone hills, that its population can exceed 7,000. Almost all the houses are mud, the exception being a few stone or brick houses belonging to traders, and, of course, the residence of the governor; but even these are mud-plastered outside, and not distinguishable by height from the crowd of inferior buildings around them. There is a poor bazaar, roofed only for some 60 yards, and this again has been built within the last three years. Great plenty of *abambars* raise their domes all over the town. There has been a mud wall, but it was never strong, and has now vanished for the most part. The town is in good repair, and fairly clean, and some of its merchants trading with Bombay *viâ* Lingah, Bandar Abbas, and Tahiir are in very comfortable circumstances. Imperfect Hindustani is spoken by a few travelled individuals."—The *Pioneer*, June 1881.

[9] *Voy. de Chirdin en Perse, &c.* Amsterdam. 1711. 4to T. II., p. 92, or 12mo. T. IV., p. 279.

conquest of the country by Abbas the Great, for Chirdin adds: "Comme on n'en bat plus depuis la conquête du royaume, on n'en voit plus guères, mais on ne laisse pas de compter par cette monnoye en tout ce pais là, et aux Indes, le long du Golfe de Cambay, et dans le pais qui en sont proche. On dit qu'elle avoit cours autrefois dans tout l'Orient."[10] In India the larym was struck by the Adil Shahi dynasty of Bijapur; several of whose specimens are preserved in different museums. One of these coins bears a distinct date, which is 1071 of Hejira, which is equivalent to 1659 A.D. The following legends, which are stamped upon these pieces of money, being incomplete, can be rendered legible or entire only by collation. They are on one side سلطان علی عادل شاہ (Sultan Ali Adil Shah), and on the other ضرب لاري دانكه سكر (Zarb Lari Dangh Sikka).[11] Here the word *dangh* is evidently *tanga*, whose origin has already been explained, while *sikka* only means "a coining die," and also a certain weight, or a standard for other weights in India. It is supposed that this coin is an imitation of the Arab طويلر (*tovylah*) from طويل (*tovyl*) 'long,' originally confined to the province of Ḥaṣa, where they are still seen, although of copper, mentioned by Palgrave and others.

The *larim* consisted of a piece of thick silver wire, something more than three inches in length, a round thread as thick as a writing quill, bent double in its length to the breadth of from one to three inches, and then slightly flattened to receive an impression. Tavernier is the only writer who mentions a *larin* and its half (which seems to be a broken piece), the division taking place at the angle, giving at the same time engravings of both the *larin* and *demi-larin*.[12] Other writers speak of the unit alone, but of two forms, viz., straight and bent. This latter variety is doubled into the shape of a fish-hook, hence known by the name of 'hook-money' or 'fish-hook money.' It has a small mark, or a chequered pattern of the prince who issued it, stamped upon it. These pattern-stamps are supposed to have some mythological meaning, and are not merely a chance ornamental device, especially those of Ceylon, where they are known by the name of *Dudu-massu*, or in the low country

---

[10] *Ibid.* Amsterdam edition of 1711. 12mo. T. IV., p. 279. *Cf.* Harris's Collection, Vol. II., p. 479.

[11] *Cf. The Numismatic Chronicle.* Lond. 1854. Vol. XVI., pp. 179 *et seq.*

[12] *Les Six Voyages de J. B. Tavernier*, between 1625 and 1664. A la Haye, 1718. Vol. II., pp. 589.

dialect *coco-ridi*, meaning 'hook-money.' [13] Ribeiro, in his *History of Ceylon*, informs us that the Portuguese, who first obtained a footing in Ceylon as early as 1517, introduced into the island the use of pagodas, pardaos, and *larins*, besides striking there their own *tangas* with the royal coat-of-arms on one side, and the image of a friar on the other, of the value of 9*d*., half-tangas and fanams.

As the description given by Tavernier of the *Larin* and the circumstances under which it was used are interesting, I insert here the following extracts :—

"Quoy qu'à Ormus et en d'autres ports du Golfe qui sont au Roy de Perse, comme l'isle de Bahren ou se fait la pesche et la vente des perles on fasse les payments en Abassis, on n'y parle toutefois que de *Larins*.

"Le *Larin* est une ancienne monnoye de Balsare et d'Arabie, et qui a cours jusqu'à l'isle de Ceylan, où l'on ne parle que de *Larins*. Cette monnoye est un fil d'argent plié en deux, de la grosseur d'un tuyau de plume ordinaire, et long de deux travers de doigt ou environ. Sur ce fil d'argent ainsi plié on voit le nom du Prince dans les pays duquel cette mon a esté fabriquée. Le huit *Larins* font un *or*, et les quatre-vint *Larins* un toman." [14]

With regard to the antiquity of this coinage nothing certain is yet known. In the absence of authentic information on this subject, the following extract from a writer who had occasion to observe the currency and note its peculiarities may be of some interest. Tavernier says :— "Au reste, le Larin est une des ancienne monnoyes de l'Asie, et bien qu'aujourd'huy elle n'ait cours que dans les Arabies et à Balsara; neanmoins, depuis Bagdat jusques dans l'Isle de Ceylan tout le negoce se fait par Larins, et surtout le long du Golfe Persique, ou l'on prend 80 Larins pour un toman qui est 50 Abassis." [15]

This coin seems, indeed, to have originally been struck at a remote era, as the type and simplicity of the style testify. All attachable pieces of money are an irrefragable proof of the comparatively rude state of society of the people who use it as a medium of exchange. The *larim*, then, not unlike the penannular ring of the ancient Celtic tribes, the Pharaohnic perfect ring in Egypt, the Chinese perforated money, and the monetary system of a simple and homely character prevailing even

---

[13] Harris's Collection, *ut supra*.

[14] *Les Six Voyages, ut supra*, Vol. I., pp. 135-136.

[15] *Loc. Cit.* Vol. II., p. 590.

at the present day for the purpose of exchange or barter, or as a representative of property in all transactions of traffic and payment, among some African races, bespeak an origin of a remote antiquity, or else of a currency in a low uncivilized condition. They are a connecting link in the ancient fabric of money, or a low stage of progress towards a full development of the beautiful medal money. But even when the minting of that particular coin has ceased, the new currency still continues, from attachment to old habits and traditions, to maintain and preserve the ancient shape or form, as is the case with the Chinese, who, though arrived at a higher stage of monetary progress, when medallic form of round discs of metal with a stamped and inscribed surface is used, still they have it perforated in the centre with a square hole, to be threaded or strung upon a cord, or slid upon a square rod of wood, or made with a suspensory ring or loop at the top of it, to suspend it from the owner's girdle for convenient carriage and safe custody.[16]

It appears that although the larim had ceased to be current in Persia for some time antecedent to the conquest of Laristan by Shah Abbas the Great, still the people used to reckon by it, so established was this coin in their estimation. In India it was mentioned, if not as a currency in use, at least as money of account as late as 1711 A.D.[17] The larim was always of pure silver, and to prove its fineness it was the custom to heat it red-hot in the fire and put it into water. If it was not pure white, it ceased to be current money. Some of the specimens of this silver-wire money, especially of the hook-variety, bore one or two notches on the edge, which seem to have been made to test the standard of the metal. The weight of the larim varied from 68½ to 72 troy grains. The Portuguese chroniclers of the 16th century attached a high degree of value to the purity or fineness of this coin, its silver being then sold at nine pardaos the mark or 8 ounces. It was originally minted without any alloy. The Portuguese made use of the word *larim*, not unlike the Muhamadans of the word *tangah* or *tanké*, for two purposes, both as a metrical and a monetary expression.

---

16 For more information on this subject, see *Numismatic Chronicle*, Vol. XI., p. 170; Vol. XII., 1849-50, pp. 89 *et seq*; Vol. XIII., 1850-51.

17 *Numismatic Chronicle*, 1854, Vol. XVI., p. 181. Also pp. 131, 159 and 165. The Portuguese chroniclers segregate *larym de Persia* from *larym* simple, the difference between the two implying that the latter was struck in India.

When they wrote one *larim* of copper and two and a half of silver, a weight of nearly 72 grains was meant, but the tanga *larim* was the coin itself. At a somewhat later date, when the coin ceased to be struck, larim became, like the *tanga branca*, a term of computation, or money of account.

Among other travellers of the 17th century, François Pyrard de Laval, who was at Goa for a couple of years from June 1608, describes the larim as current (see *Viagem*, translated by J. H. da Cunha Rivara, New Goa, 1858, Vol. I., p. 193,) at the Maldive Islands and at Goa, saying of the former that the king commands its issue, inscribing his name in Arabic letters; and Pietro della Valle, who travelled in the course of the years 1622 to 1624 along the Western Coast, speaks at length of the coin *lari*, describing its shape as *bizarra* or 'whimsical' (see *Viaggi*, Venetia, 1667, Part II., page 577). His description of the coin is worth consulting, and, in spite of my reluctance to give a long string of quotations, which render the reading generally tedious, it is so interesting that I shall close the subject of the larim with it. He describes it as a "verghetta di argento, di peso determinato, addoppiata inegualmente, e nella piegatura dove si adoppia, segnata sopra con un tantino d' impronto. Si chiama Lari, perche era moneta propria de Principi di Lar, da loro inventata, quando eran separati dal Regno della Persia. Ma per la sua bontà, e per la difficultà del falsificarsi: consistendo il suo valore solamente nel peso, e nella purità incorrotta dell' argento; è riuscita moneta, in tutto l' Oriente, tanto accetta, che nõ solo i Chani di Lar, che ne furono gli autori, ma l' han battuta poi, la batton continuamente, tutti i Principi dell' Asia, e Turchi, e Persiani, e Mogholi, e altri, con ritenerne sempre, in ogni luogo, il suo vero eprimiero nome: nè vi è moneta, in somma, in tutte queste parti, che corra più di questa: valendo a punto, ogni cinque Lari, una Piastra, ò Patacca di Reali di Spagna, ò Pezza da otto."[18]

Before dismissing the subject of what may be called the philology of numismatics, I may refer here in short to two other terms, one of which, though current even at the present time amongst the British, was originally Portuguese. It is the word *pagoda*. That eminent numismatologist, Mr. Thomas, of London, speaking of this coin, says:—"The name of this coin among Europeans is 'pagoda;' a Portuguese

---

[18] *Opus Cit.*, pp. 577-78. For the book-money of Ceylon, see the *International Numismata Orientalia*. Lond. 1879. *Ancient Coins and Measures of Ceylon.* By Mr. Rhys Davids, pp. 33 *et seq.*

appellation derived from the pyramidal temple depicted on one side of it."[19] Now there are several varieties of this gold coin, differing in type and module, their weight, assay and value being also variable. Thus the old pieces vary in weight from 60 to 120 grains troy, which is supposed to show some connection with the drachma and diadrachma of gold of the ancient Greeks, while the device and symbols of many of the old Hindû coins are said to confirm the testimony of a direct descent from a Bactrian prototype. I refrain from entering on the discussion of such a subject, which is beyond the scope of this paper.

And with regard to the origin of the word *pagoda*, it must be observed that the Portuguese on their arrival in India found here several kinds of this coin in use in the country, each under a special denomination, some of them belonging to the former rulers of the places they had conquered, and others issued from the mints of the petty ràjas or chieftains of the Malabar and Carnatic. The former were by them called *gadianacas* and *dramos*, and the latter *pagodes*. The term *dramo* may perhaps be traced to *dharan*, one of the divisions of the Hindû metrical system, equal to 3200 ratis or 10 nishkas, while *gadianaca* is certainly derived from *gadhyanam*, a weight stated in the *Lîlâvatî* (an Indian work on mathematics) to be equal to 48 *gunjas* or red *abrus precatorius* seed, each gunja averaging about two grains troy.[20] Amidst so many denominations, which the Portuguese were averse to employ in their monetary transactions, they adopted the

---

19 Prinsep's *Ind. Ant.*, *ut supra*. Vol. II., U. T., p. 17.

20 The metrical system in use in Southern India is as follows:—

2 gunjas are equal to... 1 dugala.
1 dugala is „ ... 1 fanam.
2 fanams are „ ... 1 dharana.
2 dharanas „ ... 1 hoṇa, such as máda or pratápa.
2 hoṇṇas „ ... 1 varaha or hûn or pagoda.

The chronicles of the first two centuries of the Portuguese dominion in India mention only pagodes and pardaos, but not *madas*, a Telegu term for half-pagodas. Mention is made of *son-toco* (Śuvarṇa-ṭanka), and *Rám-toco* (Râma-ṭanka), 'the stamped gold coin of Ráma,' with various symbols; amongst others those of *padma* or 'lotus' and *Śaṅkha* or 'sacred conch-shell' are not uncommon. They were probably introduced into the country from the neighbouring princes of Banavâsi first and of Vijayanagara afterwards.

In the *New Conquests* or provinces annexed to the Goa territory only about a hundred years ago, the accounts were kept until lately in sanvoy and nixany pagodes, each of them being divided into 2 pratáps, one pratáp into 5 damos, a damo into 4 pagos, a pago into 4 visvos, and a visvo into 4 cannos. The value of these pagodes was nearly 6 xerafins.

simple plan of designating all the gold coins of the Hindu princes by the generic name of *pagode*, having regard to the Hindû religious symbols on their obverse, which were either the figures of Śiva and Pârvatî and a device of the varâha (वराह), a wild boar, one of the avatârs of Vishṇu, or a representation of a temple, of an elephant, &c. Now *pagode* in Portuguese means a Hindû temple, and it was most probably the representation of a temple or an idol on the coins that induced the early Portuguese to name them in this fashion. This word may be traced to the Pâli *dagoba* (Sk. *dâthu-garbha*, 'receptacle of relics,' or *dâthu-gopa*, 'hole of relics'), the Buddhist shrine, which instead of being pyramidal, is an arched, dome-like monument.

The Muhammadans on their side appear to have simplified the process of monetary nomenclature by coining a generic term of their own to apply to the whole series of gold coins bearing on one side the effigies of Durgâ, Vishṇû, the Swâmis, and other saints, to avoid the inconvenience of especial designations which the natives of Southern India were in the habit of employing in their trade accounts. They used the term *hûn* (هون), which is derived from the Kanarese ಹೊಂನ (honna), and simply means 'gold.' To this source may now be traced not only the modern Kanarese *honnu*, the designation of half a pagoda, but also, perhaps, the word *hundi*, generally used for a bill of exchange.

One other word the Portuguese adopted from the natives of the country was *pardao*, to which they attached a value different from that of the original coin, called *pratâpa* (प्रताप), the latter being the name of the king in the legend in Devanâgarî characters on one kind of these coins. The Muhammadans had already mangled the word, calling it *partab* (پرتاب), which the Portuguese made pardao, adding *d'ouro* to mean a golden pardao, in contradistinction to the silver coin of the same designation. Although the original *pratapâ* was but the half of a pagoda, the Portuguese golden pardao was equivalent to the unit. The Portuguese eventually extended the designation of *pagodes* even to the gold mohurs issued from the mints of the Moghul emperors, calling them "pagodes de Agra," or "Agra pagodas," as distinctly mentioned in a document dated the 29th of October 1597.[21]

---

[21] *Arch. Port. Oriental.* Fasc. III., Pt. II., p. 782. By comparing the works of Abder-Razzak, who travelled in India in 1443, with those of Ludovico de Varthema, between 1504-5, the difference in the spelling of the original *pratâpa* becomes palpable. What the former writes '*pertab*' is by the latter called '*pardao*.'

In conclusion, it must be mentioned that the Portuguese never issued any pagoda of their own, as far as I am aware, and the so-called *Firingî or Porto-Novo hûns*, bearing on one side three figures, one male and two females, and on the other a merely granulated surface, as described by Marsden in his *Numismata Orientalia*, Lond. 1823, Pt. II., p. 741, were not coined under the influence of the Portuguese, but under that of the Dutch, who were their successors in the establishment at Porto Novo, up to the period of its cession to the English.

III.

I shall now pass on to consider the subject of copper and tin or tutenag coinage issued during the sixteenth century in Goa and other mint towns of the Portuguese settlements in India. But the theme is so vast in both its historical and commercial aspects, that in contemplating such a numismatic survey one is deterred at the very outset by the meagre materials whereon to build up even the bare outline of the subject. To enter into a discussion of the successive epochs, or of the serial order of mintages of the different viceroys, most of whom were in the habit of repeatedly regulating the currency, either by recalling the old coinages, supposed to have been much debased by their predecessors, which were then consigned to the crucible, and recoined

---

This writer says, moreover, of Goa, which he calls Goga, that it paid "annually to the king of Decan ten thousand golden ducats, called by them *pardai*. These *pardai* are smaller than the seraphim of Cairo, but thicker, and have two devils stamped upon one side of them, and certain letters on the other." —(*The Travels*, &c., edited by G. P. Badger, London, 1863, pp. 115-116.) It is evident from the above that prior to the Portuguese conquest of Goa the current coin of the country was the pagoda, bearing on one side the "two devils" of Varthema, which are the effigies of Śiva and Pârvati, and the legend of Śrî Kṛishṇa or Sadasiva and other kings of Vijayanagara on the other.

Barbosa, writing of Vijayanagara in 1514, says :—"The money is of gold and is called *parda* and is......coined in certain cities of this kingdom of Narsinga, and throughout all India they use this money......This coin is round, and made in a mould. Some of them have some Indian letters on one side, and two figures on the other, of a man and woman, and others have nothing but the lettering on one side."—*Descrip. of the Coasts of East Africa and Malabar.* Lond. 1866, pp. 81 and 86.)

In conclusion I must refer in short to the kind of pagoda called *varâha mudrâ*, or 'boar-stamped' gold coin, the boar being the badge of the ancient Châlukya families, as well as of the Cholars and others who issued these coins. The generic term *ora* in Konkaṇî for pagodas may be traced to this source.

into a new type and different standard; or else by altering, often without any justifiable motive, the rate of proportion between the monetised and the unwrought metals. To enter into such a discussion is, I say, easy enough from printed chronicles and even unedited official papers; but the absolute want of numismatic documents, from the extremely heedless fashion of the viceroys enforcing changes in the monetary system without even preserving in a Government cabinet the superseded specimens *ad futuram rei memoriam*, render the treatment and illustration of this part of the subject immensely difficult. However, with the aid of only a few examples, which chance has thrown in my way, having been somehow saved from the melting pot, I shall now endeavour to record in chronological order the vicissitudes this coinage has undergone, referring to historical facts embodied in the proclamations, edicts, provisions, resolutions, decrees, &c., preserved in the archives of the Government.

I have already described the copper coinage of Affonso d'Albuquerque struck in Goa and in Malacca; but only three specimens of this early mintage, viz. *leal* or *bazarucco*, *cepayqua* or *dinheiro*, and one other type of the latter, are described by Mr. Aragão at p. 113 of his work, quoting the *Lendas* of Gaspar Correa, *Decadas* of João de Barros and *Livro dos Pezos*, &c., of Antonio Nunes, as well as the *Commentarios* of Braz d'Albuquerque, the natural son of the great Portuguese hero. Of this first Portuguese coinage in India, the only specimen I have hitherto seen in India is the *cepayqua* or *dinheiro* belonging to the collection of Mr. J. M. de Sousa e Brito of Goa (see Plate III., fig. 2).

Obverse—The royal coat-of-arms, having to the left a letter resembling I.

Reverse—A sphere with a trefoil on the top. The rims are dotted.

This specimen is considerably worn out. Its weight is 50 grains troy, while the *cepayqua* described by Mr. Aragão weighs 60 Portuguese grains. The letter 'I' may be the numeral one, indicative of the value of the coin, meaning 'one cepayqua,' as conjectured by Mr. Aragão in reference to his *leal*, or it may be the initial of *India*, just as the Greek A mentioned by Gaspar Correa as inscribed on Albuquerque's *esperas* and *leues* I supposed to be the initial of Asia; but Mr. Aragão believes it to be the initial of Albuquerque's name. It seems, moreover, from statements of chroniclers, that the type of Albuquerque's coins was changed even during the short period of his governorship, which did not exceed five years.

D'Albuquerque's successor, Lopo Soares de Albergaria, was probably a party to a regulation left by Fernão de Alcaçova in 1517 for copper coinage, which left an enormous profit to the Government.[22] A quintal of copper was coined into 3,774 *reaes*, or 23¼ pardaos, a fact worth recording for comparison with subsequent issues. Diogo Lopes de Sequeira, seeing the benefit this coinage yielded to the royal treasury, decreed in 1518, and advised his successor in 1519, that the copper pieces should be freely exported, while gold and silver coinages should at first be not only forbidden to be exported, but even stopped from being struck, subsequently, in the new capital city of Goa.[23] Some reduction in the value of the copper coinage appears to have taken place during the government of Lopo Vaz de Sampaio, which ended in 1529, being succeeded by Nuno da Cunha, who ordered the issue of copper pieces, at the rate of 4 pardaos per one arroba of the metal, or one-fourth of a quintal. No specimen of this coinage has unfortunately been preserved for us.

Nuno da Cunha's successor, D. Garcia de Noronha, whose rule extended from 1538 to 1540, commanded the issue of copper *reaes* or *bazaruccos* at the rate of 18 pardaos a quintal, on account of the rise in the price of copper in the market, increasing at the same time the military pay of soldiers from four to six tangas; for tangas went in those days of frugality of living as far as rupees, just as in the Saxon period shillings went to pounds.

Mr. Aragão attributes, on account of its weight of 180 Portuguese grains, a copper real or bazarucco, having on one side the letter R or B, and on the other I, which he supposes to be either the initial of King D. João III., or the numeral one indicative of its value, to this period. But his specimen is considerably worn out, while two well-preserved specimens in my collection, apparently similar, bear the letter R on the obverse and F on the reverse, which would carry them later to the reign of one or all of the three Filippes, who sat from 1580 to 1640 on the throne of Portugal. (See Plate III., fig. 3.) Its weight is 166 grains troy, equal to 200 Portuguese grains nearly. The second specimen, which is considerably clipped, weighs only 125 grains troy. It was Martim Affonso de Sousa, who governed from 1542 to 1545, that raised for the first time the copper coinage to the exorbitant value of 36

---

22 *Arch. Port. Oriental.* Fasc. V., p. 8.

23 *Ibid.*, p. 31 and p. 19. *Ibid.*, Fasc. II., pp. 174 *et seq.*

pardaos the quintal, the market price being between 18 to 20 pardaos.[24] This was the source of all future fluctuations and troubles in the then not unimportant commercial circle of Goa.[25] We do not hear of any complaint in other settlements, although in 1544, as Gaspar Correa tells us, even the Cochin mint issued *bazaruccos* similar to those of Goa, of which fifty pieces went to one tanga.[26] Each piece weighed about 84 grains.

Such a state of things gave cause to no little discontent among the people, which found expression in representations and memorials to the Government, indicating the inconvenience and unreasonableness of the measure. A similar outcry was also raised with respect to the silver coinage a quarter of a century later. The monetary history of this period is, indeed, under an economic and financial point of view, of considerable interest even at the present day. It is extremely curious, for instance, to study by original documents the troubled state of the little commercial world, when during the viceroyalty of D. Pedro Mascarenhas, between 1554-55, the silver *patacoes* were issued, the value of which were not only in entire disproportion to the market price of the bullion, but even the coinage was debased by reducing it to the standard of billon. Such a defalcating policy of the Government gave very naturally origin to no little amount of quarrels and contentions between the Senate of Goa and the Government, resulting at the end in the Viceroy D. Antão de Noronha, between 1564 and 1568, suspending the coinage, and that extant circulating for its intrinsic worth.

But to return to the copper coinage. D. João de Castro, a man of clear intellect and fair play, reduced the abnormal rate of the copper coin of his predecessor from 36 to 25 pardaos the quintal.[27] The enthusiastic biographer of D. João de Castro, whose government extended from 1545 to 1548, gives a sensational narrative of how people came with tears in their eyes to beseech the Governor to remedy the evil by reducing the high standard of the coinage, which had enhanced the price of food, copper pieces, struck from the metal imported as merchandise from Portugal, being the currency most in use amongst Christians, Muhammadans, and Hindûs in the country.[28]

---

[24] See Mr. Aragão's *Descripção*, &c. Lisbon, 1880, p. 130.

[25] *Ibid.* Fasc. II., pp. 174—187.

[26] *Lendas da India*, Tome IV., p. 429.

[27] *Vide de D João de Castro.* By Jacinto Freire de Andrade. Paris, 1869, pp. 27-28.

[28] *Arch. Port. Oriental.* Fasc. I. Pt. I. (Second edition of 1877), p. 29.

Mr. Aragão describes the S. Thomé and pardao S. Thomé, two gold coins already mentioned by me in Part II., and a copper *bazarucco* weighing 114 Portuguese grains, all struck during the government of D. João de Castro; while a pardao S. Thomé, different from the former both in type and in weight, is attributed to his successor, Garcia de Sá.[29]

The redress of grievances about this copper question did not however last long. D. Constantino de Bragança, whose rule extended from 1558 to 1561, issued a proclamation on the 22nd of October 1559, directing that the copper coin called *tanga*, of the value of 60 reis, should be struck at the rate of 42 pardaos the quintal, the market value of the unwrought metal being only 25 pardaos.[30] The frequent fluctuations the copper coinage underwent in the course of a few years are indeed a test of the loose and unsystematic manner in which the Government treated this affair, expecting to derive from it as much profit to the treasury as was possible with the evident injury to the interests of the people. It was plainly a short-sighted policy. The rate of the copper coinage fixed by D. Constantino at 42 pardaos was by his successor, Conde de Redondo, reduced to 35, besides establishing a determined value for the whole currency of the country. But D. Antão de Noronha, who governed from 1564 to 1568, raised it again to 42, while the price of the metal was only its half. This anomaly went on for some years yet, when D. Luiz de Athayde first reduced it to 35, and then raised it again to 42 pardaos the quintal.[31] Skipping over about a decade, which is otherwise full of interest from the mass of memorials addressed by the Senate of Goa to the Government, proclamations of the viceroys, and royal letters from King D. Sebastião and Cardinal Infante, all of which throw considerable light on the subject of the gold and silver currency

---

29 *Opus Cit.*, p. 140.

30 *Arch. Port. Oriental.* Fasc. V., Pt. I., pp. 419-420.

31 It would be extremely tedious to relate in detail all these monetary alterations, and the inconvenience resulting from them to the people. The code of regulations of the mint of Goa, by D. Luis de Athayde, already referred to, is a valuable document to the numismatic history of Goa at this period. But I refrain from quoting here its extracts, from their great length. The whole document is published in the *Annaes Maritimos e Coloniaes*, Lisbon, 1844, No. 2. *Cf.* also *Memoria das Moedas*, &c., by Mr. M. B. Lopes Fernandes, Lisbon, 1856, pp. 335 *et seq.*, the work often referred to of Mr. A. C. Teixeira de Aragão, from p. 148, and the *Arch. Port. Oriental*, Fasc. I., p. 61; II., pp. 66-67. There are several other documents worth quoting, relative to the numismatic period under consideration, but they are much too long for our limits.

of the period, and especially the copper coinages which are said to have been minted by Albuquerque in 1510 at 13 pardaos the quintal, and now raised to the enormous rate of 42, I shall pass on to describe the issue of *bazaruccos*, which are, as far as I am aware, inedited. These are the copper coins described in Part II. as having on the obverse a sheaf of arrows and a bow, and on the reverse the usual coat-of-arms of the kingdom. I have already illustrated this specimen at Plate II., fig. 3, its weight being 155 grains troy. I have now to add another specimen of the same type, but weighing nearly the double of that of the former, being 305 grains troy (see Plate III., fig. 4). Now these *bazaruccos* having been issued some time prior to 1577, are probably those attributed to the viceroy Antonio Moniz Barreto, who ruled between 1573 and 1577.

Next to this type of the copper *bazarucco* one may perhaps place, without incurring the risk of an anachronism, the copper *bazaruccos* illustrated at Plate II., figs. 4 and 5; the former bearing on the obverse the letters BCCO, and the latter the numeral 15. Now these coins weigh 305 and 200 grains troy, respectively. They belong to my cabinet, as well as those of the sheaf of arrows type. I have to add now one other, also pertaining to the same collection. It bears the coat-of-arms on the obverse, and the figure 5 on the reverse (see Plate III., fig. 5). It weighs 285 troy grains. Then come the other copper *bazaruccos*, bearing letters, which are initials of the names of kings. The little copper *bazarucco* having on one side the letter S and on the other a cross, was apparently struck during the reign of King D. Sebastião, while the *bazarucco* bearing the letter F, already described, was issued during the time the Filippes of Spain were kings of Portugal. (See Plate III., fig. 3.) The little *bazarucco* of the S type weighs 45 grains troy, but it is much clipped and worn out. (See Plate III., fig. 6.) All these coins are unpublished. The arrow type *bazaruccos* were evidently struck during the reign of King D. Sebastião, from 1557 to 1578.

To pass on now to record the alterations subsequent to the year 1577 of the copper coinage, which was for many years the financial topic of the day, we find that among the successors of the viceroy Antonio Moniz Barreto, from 1577 to 1584, D. Francisco Mascarenhas is the only viceroy whose *bazaruccos*, described by Mr. Aragão at p. 168 of his work, have been preserved, and to whom the Senate of Goa presented that remarkable document containing the numismatic history of Goa from the time of Albuquerque.[32] During his government the copper coinage was minted at the rate of 57 pardaos the quintal, while its market value was only 22, and he reduced it to 47 on hearing the representation of the Senate. From 1584 to 1600 we find no innovation in the type or standard of the copper pieces, the weight of the *bazarucco* being then 123 Portuguese grains, except the issue of tin *bazaruccos*, five of which were equivalent to four of copper. From 1600 to the middle of the century we hear of constant fluctuations in the value of the copper and tin coinages, two and even three old pieces being exchanged for one new piece, on account of the low standard and introduction of false coin from the neighbouring countries into Goa, the process of fabrication being facilitated by the abundance of the metals, and the ease with which the rude colonial type of the Portuguese coinage could be imitated.

Before closing this chapter I must describe in short the prevalent types of the copper *bazaruccos*, the emission of the earliest of which has been attributed to the time of D. Filippe II. The specimen figured at Pl. III., fig. 7, has on one side the royal coat-of-arms between the letters G and A for Goa; and on the other a wheel, allusive to St. Catherine's wheel, the patron saint of Goa. This specimen belongs to the collection of Mr. J. M. de Sousa e Brito. Its weight is 50 grains troy.

Two other *bazaruccos* in my cabinet (Pl. III., figs. 8 and 9) have one the coat-of-arms between rather indistinct G and A on the obverse, and a wheel and a cross on the reverse; and the other the coat-of-arms between the letters B or R, the initials of *bazarucco* or *roda*, and another letter, which is almost invisible, on the obverse; and a cross with stars in each angle on the reverse. Their weight is 35 grains troy. Of the latter kind there are two specimens in my collection, one of them weighing 40 grains troy. None of the copper *bazaruccos* bears any date, but Mr. Aragão, at p. 273 of his work, describes a *bazarucco* bearing the year 1698, belonging to the collection of Mr. Roberto of Lisbon, and weighing 94 Port. grs. It is attributed to the time of the viceroy Camara Coutinho, who governed India from 1698 to 1701.

IV.

I shall now proceed to enumerate from authentic documents the issues of money in chronological succession under the heading of each sovereign and his viceroys in India, and to describe the coins hitherto

[32] *Arch. Port. Oriental.* Fasc. II., pp. 216-221.

preserved or known to be existing in India and elsewhere, in both public and private collections.

KING D. FILIPPE I. 1580—1598.

During the rule of this monarch, the Viceroy Fernão Telles de Menezes, who held the reins of the government of Portuguese India for a short period of only seven months, from the 10th March to the 17th September 1581, caused the mintage of *xerafins*, first issued during the sway of his predecessor, to cease altogether, as prejudicial both to the State and people.[33] His successor, D. Francisco Mascarenhas, whose rule extended until November 1584, being enlightened by the Senate of the city of Goa with a lengthy and lucid statement, already referred to, on the inconvenience resulting from frequent alterations in the standard of money, struck there from the time of D. Albuquerque onwards, confirmed the cessation of the issue of the *xerafins* of five tangas, and commanded the coinage of copper pieces with the abatement of ten pardaos in the price stipulated for on one quintal or 58,752 *kil.* of the metal. Mr. Aragão describes at page 168 of his work a *bazarucco* with the numeral 7½, weighing 134 Portuguese grains, belonging to this viceroyalty. He was followed by D. Duarte de Menezes, Conde de Tarouca, who governed until the 4th May 1588, on which date he died. His share in the monetary history of Goa is confined to the reissue of the silver *xerafins*, of which no specimen is now available.[34] His successors in a series of years from 1588 to 1617 appear to have avoided interfering with the currency then in vogue, the only exception being Manuel de Sousa Coutinho, whose rule ended in 1591, and who is said to have decreed the issue of silver xerafins with a considerable amount of the alloy[35]; Mathias d'Albuquerque, whose sway extended up to 1597, commanded the issue of coins in four metals, although, with the exception of his silver tanga, described at page 177 by Mr. Aragão in his work, no specimen of his coinage has been preserved. He also attempted to fix the price of gold S. Thomés at eight tangas and a half each[36]; and D. Francisco da Gama, Conde da Vidigueira, the grand-

---

[33] *Arch. Port. Oriental.* Nova Goa, 1857. Fasc. II., p. 219.

[34] Fasc. I., p. 2.

[35] *Livro de Mon.*, MS., fol. 346.

[36] Fasc. III., Pt. II., p. 783. With regard to the first issue of S. Thomés, which F. N. Xavier and others attribute to Garcia de Sá's rule, Aragão places it in the period of the government of D. João de Castro. See *Opus Cit.*, p. 137.

son of the great navigator, Vasco da Gama, who returned to Lisbon in 1600, did nothing more than to forbid the circulation of the pagodas of less than 43 *pontas*, or 20¼ carats, in the country.[37] In the meantime King D. Filippe I. died, and was succeeded by D. Filippe II.

D. Filippe II. 1598—1621.

The circulation of the pagodas, which had by the former viceroy been suspended, was now, in the year 1598, resumed by the Conde da Vidigueira. Of his successors, Ayres de Saldanha, D. Martim Affonso de Castro, D. Fr. Aleixo de Menezes, André Furtado de Mendonça, and D. Jeronymo de Azevedo, from 1600 to 1617, we have only specimens of coinage struck during the government of the last, all the other viceroys having left us but some dry written documents relating to that interminable question of copper and tin *bazaruccos*, and their enhanced circulating value in relation to the price of the corresponding metals in the market. The last viceroy appears, moreover, to have nearly put an end to this affair by his provision, dated the 11th of June 1616, enforcing the issue of tutenag *bazaruccos* at the actual price of that amalgam, with the addition of six pardaos for the cost of mintage.[38] Of the coins struck during the government of D. Jeronymo de Azevedo, there were silver tangas, its multiples and divisions, besides the copper and tutenag *bazaruccos*. A contemporary writer, Manoel Barboza, in his work entitled *Remissiones Doctorum, &c.*, printed at Lisbon in 1618, describes the coins current in Portuguese India thus :—" Gold Coins :—*Gold pardao* of 18 carats, value from 320 to 340 reis. *Gold S. Thomés* of 18 carats, weighing 1250 (?). Those struck by the order of viceroys in India are worth 10 tangas or 600 reis. The *Venetians* (sequins) are current in India, being introduced from Venice to Ormuz and other eastern countries. They are worth from 11½ to 12 tangas, or from 690 to 720 reis. Then the *pagodes*, of the value of 9½ to 10 tangas, or from 570 to 600 reis. Silver Coins :—*Leal*, worth 12 reis, but no document is yet found relating to the issue of this kind of coin. *Tanga* is worth 60 reis. *Salares*, Persian coin brought from Ormuz, the value of each being about 90 reis. *Xerafins* or *bastiões* are coins struck in India by the command of viceroys, of the

---

[37] Fasc. III., Pt. II., p. 782.

[38] *Livro de Alvarás*. MS. II., fol. 21. *Arch. Port. Oriental.*, Fasc. I., Pt. II., pp. 218, 224, 228.

value of 300 reis."[39] It is apparent from the enumeration of coins above that the writer alludes to the currency of the country some years prior to the publication of his book, for in 1618 the *bastiões* had ceased to pass current. Pyrard, in 1608, says :—"First, there are the so-called *bazaruccos*, of which 75 go to a *tanga*. Then there are old *bazaruccos*, of which 115 are equal to one tanga. Lower than this coin are small unstamped copper pieces, called *Arco*, of which 240 go to a *tanga*. Of these coins one is of iron and the other of *calaim*, a metal from China."[40] In 1611 *bazaruccos* were struck at Bassein and Damaun.[41]

Of silver tangas, coined during the viceroyalty of D. Jeronymo de Azevedo, and which are by some writers attributed to that of the Conde de Linhares, only three specimens have been preserved, one at Lisbon and the others at Goa. The former is described in the *Hist. Gen.* Tome VI., p. 346, where also the law of 20th March 1617 for the city of Goa to cease striking the tutenag and tin *bazaruccos*, but to coin only, in case of need, those of copper, as was decreed in 1605, and still earlier in 1583, is given in full.[42] The latter are described in the above quoted *Memoria* of Mr. F. N. Xavier, p. 80 (see Plate III., fig. 10).

Obverse—In the field the royal coat-of-arms, with the monetary mark M. T., one letter on each side, the marginal inscription being F. II., R. P., *i.e.*, *Filippus II.*, *Rex Portugaliæ.*

Reverse—A cross on Calvary, the legend around being. I. H. S. V., *i. e.*, *In Hoc Signo Vinces*, a motto, in reference to the cross, adopted by the Portuguese on their coinage of the kingdom, years before. Its weight is 30 Portuguese grains.

The mint mark M. T. means, according to Mr. F. N. Xavier, Malacca Tanga, which, in conformity with the Government resolution dated the 27th August 1631, was ordered to be struck. Although it bears the name of D. Filippe II., it was in reality coined in the reign of his successor, the resolution above referred to determining that the type should be similar to that of the preceding years. The example in the cabinet of the late Mr. Xavier bears on one side the legend *in extenso*, and the letters I. T., or 'one tanga.' Its weight

[39] Fasc. V., Pt. I., p. 327.

[40] *Opus Cit.* Vol. II., pp. 55 *et seq.*

[41] Fasc. VI., pp. 870, 976.

[42] *Memoria das Moedas Correntes em Portugal, &c.* By M. P. Lopes Fernandes. Lisbon. 1856 Vol. I., p. 176.

is Port. 30 grains, equal to 25 troy grains. I may mention here, once for all, that the relation of these two kinds of weight to the metrico-decimal system is as follows:—One gramme = Port. grains 20·07843, and English troy grains 15.

Mr. Aragão at pp. 196—198 of his work, describes a *tanga* and *meia tanga*, struck during this government, explaining the letters M. T. to mean *meia tanga*. He also describes two copper pieces of one and five *bazaruccos*. Silver specimens weigh 60 and 29 Portuguese grains respectively, while of the copper coins, that of five *bazaruccos* weighs 289 grains, and of one *bazarucco* 58.

De Azevedo's successor, D. João Coutinho, Conde de Redondo, whose rule extended from November 1617, to November 1619, had a great deal to do with the rate of exchange of the tin, tutenag and copper coinage of *bazaruccos*. He also decreed the issue of silver *bazaruccos*, of which only two specimens have been preserved, of 30 and 10 *bazaruccos*, the latter described by Mr. Aragão at p. 201 of his work, from the collection of the late Mr. F. N. Xavier. For a specimen of the *bazarucco* 30, see Pl. IV., fig. 11. It belongs to the collection of Mr. Sousa e Brito. No specimen of 20 *bazaruccos* has been hitherto found. The 30 *bazaruccos* has on the obverse the coat-of-arms of the kingdom, and on the reverse the numeral 30, indicative of its value of 30 *bazaruccos*, the rim being beaded all round. Its silver is 11 dinheiros in fineness, and weight 15 grains troy.[43]

On the death of the Conde de Redondo, Fernão de Albuquerque, who governed up to December 1622, ordered the minting of *bazaruccos* at a more reasonable rate. It was during his rule that King D. Filippe II. died, being succeeded by D. Filippe III. on the 8th of April 1621.

D. Filippe III. 1621—1640.

The successors of Fernão de Albuquerque, D. Francisco da Gama and D. Fr. Luis de Brito, have left no new type of coinage. The former, however, issued several provisions regulating the value of coins in circulation, which documents have fortunately been preserved. It was however reserved for their successor, and one of the most distinguished viceroys Portuguese India ever had, to cause considerable

---

[43] For documents relating to this coinage, see *Arch. Port. Oriental*, Fasc. VI., pp. 1180 *et seq.*

LÂMINA IV

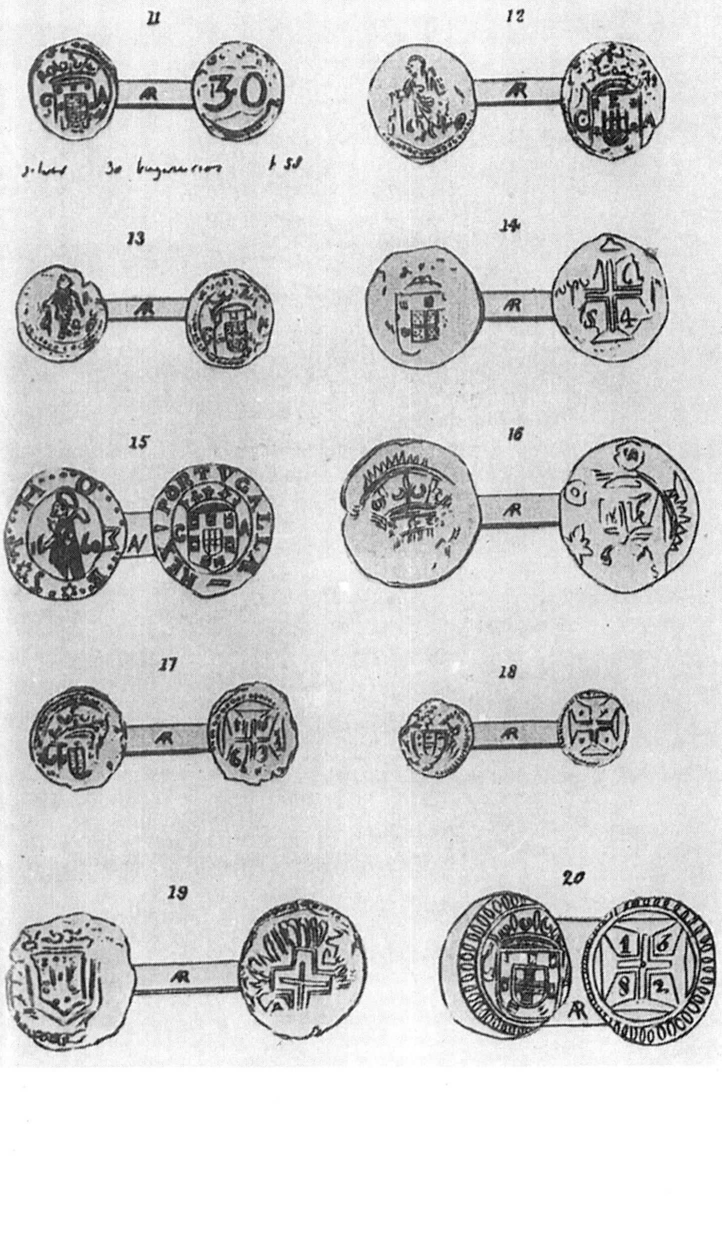

alteration in the coinage of the country. This was D. Miguel de Noronha, Conde da Linhares, whose beneficent rule extended from October 1629 to December 1635. On the 13th November 1630, he commanded the issue of the new silver coinage of the standard of *reales* or dollars, under the designation of *patacões* of the value of six tangas, *meios* or half *patacões*, *tangas*, and *half tangas*, the weight of the *patacão* being fixed at 345 Portuguese grains, and value at 360 reis, that of the remaining coins being regulated in proportion to this, the fundamental unity of the new monetary scheme.[44] Then on the 5th November 1631, gold S. Thomés, of the standard of 39½ points, and value of three xerafins and twelve reis, were struck, having on one side a cross and on the other the numeral 912, their value in reis; while the pagodas of 38 points, weight 66¾ Portuguese grains, were allowed to circulate at the value of 14 tangas and 12 reis.[45] The issue of the gold S. Thomés gave rise to a new denomination and to a controversy. As they bore no effigy of the saint in whose honour they were first struck, the two varieties were known by the name of *Santomés velhos* and *Santomés novos*, or 'old' and 'new' S. Thomés. The controversy arose with the Court of Portugal from the suppression of the figure of the saint, and stamping instead a cross, which was of the order of S. Bento, the viceroy being one of its knights. The viceroy explained that it was not personal vanity that had induced him to stamp the cross of the Order to which he belonged, but only the desire to produce a new type, and in accordance with the practice prevailing during former viceroyalties, when pieces of money bearing new designs, such as the images of S. Sebastian and S. Philip, were coined. The new coinage was however forbidden, a royal edict ordaining that S. Thomés should in the future bear the impress of the saint on the obverse, having on the reverse the Cross of the Order of Christ, of which the king was Grand Master, and to which allegiance in the form of a certain amount of pecuniary tribute was paid in the country. His silver coinage was also suspended, his gold coinage only remaining, struck in 1634, and styled *xerafim* and *half xerafim*, of the standard of old S. Thomés, their value being 300 and 150 reis respectively. They were admitted into circulation at Goa, Cochin, and Malacca.[46]

---

[44] *Livro de M.* IV., fol. 125.

[45] *L. de M.* No. 104, p. 242.

[46] See *Memoria, &c., ut supra*, pp. 80-82. Navarrette, writing about the middle of the seventeenth century, says:—"The coin that passed at Colombo

Of the silver money issued by the viceroy, Conde de Linhares, only two specimens have been preserved, belonging to the collection of the University of Leyden. They are described and illustrated by Mr. Aragão at pp. 218 *et seq.* of his already mentioned work.

His successor, Pedro da Silva, whose rule extended from December 1635 to the 24th of June 1639, decreed by a resolution, dated the 16th of January 1637, that silver money of the standard of the *tostao*, struck in Portugal, should be issued, consisting of *xerafins*, weighting 312½ Portuguese grains, *meio xerafim*, *tanga* of the weight of 62½ grains, and *meia tanga*.[47]

But now a new era dawned for Portugal and her dependencies. The Portuguese had long borne with inimitable patience the weight of the Spanish yoke, which had, by depriving them of their former glorious conquests, atoned in part at least for their past guilty career in the Eastern land and sea. A plot long formed now broke out; and the Spanish ruler being driven away, the grandson of the Duke of Bragança, who had been deprived of his right by Philip II. of Spain, was in 1640 proclaimed king, under the title of D. João IV. But on ascending the throne, the sovereign of Portugal, now become once more independent, found his vast ultramarine empire a mere wreck. Such a retribution for an egoistical and overbearing policy in India, barring of course some brilliant acts of valour and heroism, was indeed far above the wages of their misdeeds. But to return to numismatics.

Although the dynastic change took place in 1640, it would seem that in those days of slow navigation the news was not known in India, or else a party favorable to Philip of Spain continued to govern India; for as late as the following year coins were struck bearing the effigy of S. Philip, in honor of the king of that name. Reference will be made to the coinage struck in this year in the sequel, but it is time to describe here the two following specimens of silver coins struck in 1640. (See Plate IV., figs. 12 and 13.)

Obverse—The effigy of S. Filippe with a long cross in the right hand between the letters S. F. (S. Filippe), and below the year 1640.

Reverse—The coat-of-arms of the kingdom, with the monetary mark G. A. The former of these specimens weighs 65 grs. troy, and the latter 32½ grs. They belong to the collection of Mr. Sousa e Brito.

---

was vize-dollars, rupees, and S. Thomas's pagodes, pieces of eight, and a particular coin for the country like that they had at Malaca."—*Churchill's Collection of Voyages*, Lond. 1732, Vol. I., p. 272.

[47] *Liv.* V., p. 219.

D. Joao IV. 1640—1656.

The last viceroy of the late monarch of the dynasty of the Philips of Spain, Antonio Telles de Menezes, who governed from 1639 to 1640, issued silver *xerafins* and *tangas* with their halves, described by Mr. Aragão at pp. 225-226 of his book. The first viceroy of the new reign of D. João IV., João da Silva Tello de Menezes, whose rule ended in December 1645, appears to have retained, without any considerable alteration, the monetary system in vogue during the viceroyalty of his immediate predecessors, changing, however, the effigy of S. Philip for that of S. John, a childish flattery keenly appreciated by kings rather than by saints, whose figures the coins bore. His successor, D. Filippe Mascarenhas, in the government of India from 1645 to 1651, by the deliberation of the Council of the State Treasury, issued on the 14th of January 1646 a new silver coinage for circulation at Mozambique, called *crusados* of the value of 400 reis, of the standard and fineness of the *xerafins* cerrent in the country, and of the weight of the *patacões* struck in 1630,[48] while all gold bullion from China and Mozambique imported into Goa was ordered to be taken over to the mint for coining S. Thomés of the standard of old S. Thomés, of the value of 4 *xerafins* and half *tanga* apiece.[49] In 1649, by the decree dated the 15th June, more silver *xerafins* of the standard of those current were struck,[50] and in 1650, by the resolution of the 18th February, silver *xerafins* with a new type, consisting of, instead of the figure of S. John, which was impressed in honour of the reigning monarch, the Cross of the Order of Christ on one side, and the royal coat-of-arms on the other, its weight being 211 Portuguese grains, while that of the *pardao* hitherto current was 220 grains, and 25 *vintens* in value, each vintem of 12 *reis*.[51]

One of these pieces, bearing date 1654, is in my cabinet.

Obverse—The royal coat-of-arms.

Reverse—The Cross of the Order of Christ, with the date 1654 in its angles. (Plate IV., fig. 14.) Weight 78 grains troy.

Of the successors of the viceroy, Dom Filippe Mascarenhas, D. Rodrigo Lobo da Silveira, Conde de Sarzedas, was the only one, in the

---

[48] *Liv.* VI., fol. 153. The silver used in the manufacture of this coinage was obtained from Japan, and from 100,000 dollars paid by the Dutch in satisfaction of one of the stipulations of the peace treaty.

[49] *Ibid.*, p. 120.

[50] *Ibid.*, VIII., folio 76.

[51] *Liv. de Moncões*, 22, fol. 14.

course of ten years, from 1650 to 1660, to issue the tin coinage of *bazaruccos*, which was continued by the succeeding governors. Mr. Aragão also informs us that during his government were issued three silver coins—viz., *xerafins*, *meios xerafins*, and *tangas*, two of which he describes at p. 238 of his work. In this interval King D. João died, on the 6th of November 1656, and was succeeded by D. Affonço VI.

D. Affonso VI. 1656—1667.

In 1660 was issued, according to Tavernier, the gold S. Thomé of the value of four rupees, of which he gives an illustration in his book of travels.

Obverse—Area is occupied by the figure of S. Thomas, with a nimbus round the head, and club on left shoulder, and the year 1660. In the margin S. TOME.

Reverse—The area contains the royal coat-of-arms with the mint mark G—A (Goa), and the margin has the words *Rex Portugaliæ*. (Plate IV., fig. 15.)

This engraving has also been copied by both Mr. Lopes Fernandes, Vol. I., p. 208 of his work before mentioned, on the coins current in Portugal from the time of the Romans to 1856, and by Mr. Aragão at Pl. II., fig. 10. Now among the documents existing in the archives of the Goa Secretariat, there is no mention made of this type, and as Tavernier is known to have been one of those travellers endued with a powerful imagination, one may perhaps be justified in doubting of such a coin having ever been in circulation. The engravings furnished, for instance, by this writer of the zodiacal series of coins of the Emperor Jahângîr, are not merely ill-designed and incorrect, but have little analogy to the originals, as Marsden has demonstrated in his *Numismata Orientalia*, Lond. 1823, Pt. II., p. 612. But as the description given of the Portuguese currency in India by the author has some historical interest, I append it here below :—

" La monnoye d'or que les Portugais font batre à Goa est à meilleur tître que nos Louys d'or, et pese un grain plus que notre demi-pistole. Du temps que j'etois à Goa cette piece valoit quatre roupies, ou six francs de nostre monnoye. Ils la tiennent ainsi haute afin que les marchands qui viennent de tous les costez des Indes leur apporter des marchandises, ne transportent point hors du pais leur monnoye d'or, et ils appellent cette piece *Saint Thomê*......Ils ont aussi des pièces d'argent, qu'ils appellent *Pardos* (pardaos) et qui passent pour la valeur de 27 sols de notre monnoye ; comme aussi quantité de petite monnoye de cuivre et d'estain."[52]

The next 10 years, from 1660 to 1670, do not show us any considerable alteration in the coinages above referred to, except a silver *tanga*, struck during the government of Antonio de Mello de Castro, and described by Mr. Aragão at p. 247 of his book.

During the viceroyalty of João Nunes da Cunha, Conde de S. Vicente, whose rule extended from October 1666 to November 1668, it was forbidden, by a decree dated the 9th July 1667, to admit any foreign coinage of copper, tin, or tutenag, into the dependencies of Chaul, Bassein, and Damaun, only the ancient and modern *bazaruccos* struck at Goa being allowed to circulate, and silver *xerafins* were issued on the 28th November 1668, weighing 211 Portuguese grains apiece, the value of a mark of silver being coined into 21 *pardaos*, 4 *tangas*, and 12 *reis*. He also forbade the use of debased pagodes, except those of Barcelor, called *sanagaris pataxa* and the *agramutes* (? Agra muhrs). In the meantime D. Affonço was succeeded by King D. Pedro, who ruled from 1667 to 1706.

D. Pedro II. 1667—1706.

The Viceroy Conde de Lavradio commanded in 1672 the issue of silver xerafins from old dollars of the same weight and standard as those coined on the 21st November 1668, and fixed the standard of both gold and silver coinages, which were fluctuating for some years, from the intrinsic value of the metals not being equal to their conventional or legal values, and from the officers of the mint being extremely arbitrary in their mint regulations, while D. Fr. Antonio Brandão and Antonio Paes de Sande restored in 1670 the value of the gold S. Thomés, slightly altered by their predecessors, to that of five xerafins, caused the mintage of tin money to cease from the 11th January 1680, and ordered all the silver *abbâssis* and *mahmûdîs* brought from Persia to be taken as so much bullion over to the mint to be coined into *xerafins*, weighing 211 Port. grains apiece, *tangas*, and half *tangas*, from February 1681.[53] Mr. Aragão describes at p. 255 of his work a silver S. Thomé, bearing the date 1672, and at p. 258 *meia tanga* and five *bazaruccos* struck during the years 1678 and 1679. The

[52] *Les Six Voyages, &c.*, 1718. Tome II., pp. 614-615.

[53] *Liv. de Mon.* XIV., fol. 103.

specimens of the silver coinage of this period are extremely rare. The following are, as far as I am aware, unique—

Obverse—The coat-of-arms of the kingdom.

Reverse—Area, the cross of the Order of Christ, with the year 1664, rather indistinct, in the angles. On the margin the letter S, the T being invisible, the two letters being initials of S. Thomé. Then there are two countermarks round the edge resembling an O and a star, made probably at the readjustment of the coin. This specimen is in my collection. Weight 156 grains troy. (Plate IV., fig. 16.)

Mr. Aragão, at p. 247 of his work, describes a silver tanga bearing the date 1665, supposed to have been struck for the province of Bassein.

A piece of two *tangas* in silver :—

Reverse—The Cross of the Order of Christ in the field, and within a beaded rim, having the year 1663 in the angles.

Obverse—The royal coat-of-arms within a similar circle, with the mint mark G—A (Goa). Weight 30 grains troy. (Plate IV., fig. 17.)

Then there is the silver tanga :—

Reverse—The Cross of the Order of Christ within the border, as in the above specimen, with four stars in the angles of the cross.

Obverse—The royal coat-of-arms. Weight 18 grains troy. (Plate IV., fig. 18.) The two tangas above described belong also to my collection.

From 1670 to 1680 we have no document reporting any alteration in the monetary system in vogue. As for the specimens of the coins struck between 1678 and 1880, Mr. Aragão describes, as already mentioned, a silver tanga, bearing the date 1678, belonging to the collection of the late Mr. F. N. Xavier of Goa, and a copper coin of the value of five *bazaruccos*. It was during the rule of the Viceroy Conde de Alvôr, from 1681 to 1686, that both gold and silver coins were issued, called St. Thomé, xerafim, meio xerafim, and tanga, all of which are described at pp. 262-263 of Mr. Aragão's book. A peculiarity worth noting about the type of the silver xerafim and tanga is the substitution of the Cross of the Order of Christ, which was prevalent in former issues, by that of St. George. (See Plate IV., fig. 19.)

Obverse—The coat-of-arms of the kingdom.

Reverse—The Cross of St. George, with various ornaments all round. Weight 232 Port. grains. In my collection.

A tanga of the same type is described by Mr. Aragão at p. 263 of his work.

About this time Goa was visited by a considerably larger number of visitors than in the time of Pyrard, some of whom have noted down in their travels the coinage current in Goa. One of these seems to be Mr. William Barret, who, writing in 1684, gives of the Goa coinage a detailed account, to which I may well add the description of currencies in other Portuguese settlements at that time. But before doing so, I must allude, in short, to a silver coin which has borne the varying denomination of silver St. Thomé, xerafim and rupia, the last being the name now prevailing for a silver coin of that standard. There are several specimens of it bearing the date from 1682 to 1689. (See Plate IV., fig. 20.)

Obverse—The coat-of-arms of the kingdom between the letters G. A., its monetary mark.

Reverse—The Cross of the Order of Christ, with the year 1682, the numerals in the angle of the cross. Its weight is 212 Port. grains.

" For the mony of Goa," says Mr. William Barret, " there is a kind of mony made of lead and tin mingled, being thicke and round, and stamped on the one side with the sphere or globe of the world, and on the other side two arrows and 5 rounds : and this kind of mony is called Basaruchi, and 15 of these make a vinton of naughty mony, and 5 vintons make a tanga, and 4 vintenas make a tanga of base mony ; so that the tanga of base mony is 60 basaruchies, and the tanga of good mony 75 basaruchies, and 5 tangas make a seraphine of gold, which in merchandize is worth 5 tangas good mony : but if one would change them into Basaruchies, he may have 5 tangas and 16 basaruchies which overplus they cal cerafagio, and when they bargain of the pardaw of gold, each pardaw is ment to be 6 tangas good mony, but in merchandize they use not to demand pardawes of gold in Goa, except it be for jewels and horses, for all the rest they take of seraphins of silver *per adviso.*

" The roials of plate, I say, the roial of 8 are worth per custom and commandment of the King of Portugall 400 reies, and every rey is one basaruchie and one-fourth part, which maketh tangas 6 and 53 basaruchies as their just value, but for that the said roials are excellent silver and currant in divers places of India and chiefly in Malacca, when the ships are to depart at the in due times (called Monsons) every one to have the said roials pay more than they are worth, and the overplus, as is above said, they call serafagio. And first they give the just value of the 100 roials of 8, at 5 tangas 50 basaruchies apiece, which done, they give seraphins 5, 6, 7, 8, 9, 10, 12, 15 until 22 by the 100, according as they are in request.

"The duckat of gold is worth 9 tangas and a halfe good mony, and yet not stable in price, for that when the ships depart from Goa to Cochin, they pay them at 9 tangas and three-fourth partes and 10 tangas, and that is the most that they are worth.

"The larines are worth by just value basaruchies 93 and three-fourth parts, and 4 larines make a seraphine of silver, which is 5 tangas of good mony, and these also have serafagion of 6, 7, 8, 10, untill 16, by the 100, for when the ships depart for the north, to say, for Chaul, Diu, Cambaia, or Bassaim, all carry of the same, because it is mony more currant than any other.

"There is also a sort of seraphins of gold of the stampe of Ormuz, whereof there are but fewe in Goa, but being there, they are woorth five larines and somewhat more, according as they are in request.

"There is also another litle sort of mony, round, having on the one side a crosse, and on the other side a crowne, which is woorth one halfe a tanga of good mony, and another of the same stampe lesse than that which they call Imitino de buona moneda, which is worth 18 basaruchies three-fourth parts a piece.

"Note that if a man bargaine in merchandize, it behooveth to demaund tangas of good mony : for by nominating tangas onely, is understood to be base mony of 60 basaruchies, which wanteth of the good mony *ut supra*." [64]

Writing of Cochin, he says :—"The mony of Cochin are all the same sorts which are currant in Goa, but the duckat of gold in value is 10 tangas of good mony."—*Ibid.*, p. 411.

Of Malacca he writes :—"For the mony of Malacca, the least mony currant is of tinne stamped with the armes of Portugall, and 12 of these make a chazza. The chazza is also of tinne with the said armes, and 2 of these make a challaine.

"The challaine is of tinne with the said armes, and 40 of these make a tanga of Goa good mony, but not stamped in Malacca.

"There is also a sort of silver mony which they call Patachines, and is worth 6 tangas of good mony, which is 360 reyes, and is stamped

[64] Hakluyt's Collection of the Early Travels, &c. Lond. 1810. Vol. II., p. 410.

with two letters S. T., which is S. Thomas, on one side, and the arms of Portugall on the other side.

"There is also a kind of mony called cruzados, stamped with the armes of Portugall, and is worth 6 tangas good mony, the larines are every 9 of them worth 2 cruzados, which is 12 tangas good mony, and these larines be of those which are stamped in Balsara and Ormuz. The roials of 8 they call Pardaos de Reales, and are worth 7 tangas of good mony."—*Ibid.*, p. 411.

Of Ormuz he says:—"Touching the mony of Ormuz, the bargaine in merchandize at so many leches by the barre, which lech is 100 Asaries, and maketh larines 100 and a halfe, which maketh pardaos 38, and larines one-halfe, at larines 5 by the pardao. One asarie is sadines 10, and every sadine is 100 danarie.

"The larine is worth 5 sadines and one-fourth part, so that the sadine is worth of Aleppo money 1 medine and one-fourth part, and the larine is in Balsara worth of Alleppo money 6 medines and a half.

"The pardao is 5 larines of Balsara.

"There is also stamped in Ormuz a seraphine of gold which is little and round, and is worth 24 sadines, which maketh 30 medines of Aleppo.

"The Venetian money is worth in Ormuz larines 88 per 100 meticals, and the roials are worth larines 86 lesse one sadine, which is every thousand meticals 382 asures; but those that will not sel them, use to melt them, and make them so many larines in the King of Ormuz his mint, whereby they cleare 2 per 100, and somewhat more: and this they doe because neither Venetian money nor roials were as currant in Ormuz, *per adviso*."—*Ibid.*, p. 408.

Passing on now to describe the coinage struck subsequent to 1690, we find that from that year to 1706 there was little or no change in the type or standard of the currency in use, except in readjusting copper and tutenag coins, whereby two old pieces were made equivalent to a new one, and even three to one, to which allusion has already been made.

In the meantime King D. Pedro II. died in 1706, being succeeded by D. João V., whose reign continued till 1750, and it covers by twenty years more, the rest of the period allotted to this paper.

D. João V. 1706—1750.

The first viceroy of this reign, D. Rodrigo da Costa, from 1707 to 1712, does not appear to have made any alteration in the currency, which was considerably modified by his successor, Vasco Fernandes Cesar de Menezes, who allowed, besides, private parties to send gold to the mint for coining money, a concession not apparently the first of its kind, and to receive 96 S. Thomés, of 5 xerafins each, per one mark of gold, after paying the seignorage, cost of mintage, &c.

This new issue of S. Thomés gave again rise to the denomination of *velhos e novos*, or old and new S. Thomés. He also decreed the minting of tin *bazaruccos* with an alloy of tutenag and lead in certain proportions in two distinct series of coins. To this time may perhaps be attributed the tutenag *bazarucco* illustrated at Plate V., fig. 21.

The originals of this and the following coins are in my collection. They all, with the exception of the first, the attribution of which by Mr. Aragão to the reign of D. Pedro II. is worth recording (see p. 258 of his work), weighing 130 Portuguese grains, bear dates as well as the mint mark G. A.* The other specimen, fig. 22, bears the coat-of-arms on one side, and the initial of the name of D. João V. and the numeral 15, indicative of the value of the coin in *bazaruccos*. The specimens, figs. 23 and 24, bear the date 1722, and also their value in 7½ and 5 *bazaruccos*. They weigh 180 and 152 Portuguese grains respectively. But the most curious, and hitherto inedited coin, is the tutenag specimen, discovered at Tanna some years ago while laying the foundation of a house. (See Plate V., fig. 25.) It is partly broken at the edge, but the type is fortunately entire. It bears the coat-of-arms of the kingdom, with the mint mark D. and B., which seem to stand for Damaun and Bassein, on the obverse, and the Cross of the Order of Christ on the reverse, with the year 1723 in the angles.

In conclusion, it remains to describe the silver coin bearing the portrait of King D. João V., which is so uncouth as to be styled a libel on the physiognomy of that not otherwise handsome person. It is known by the name of rupia, having its division of meia rupia or pardao, meio pardao, tanga, e meia tanga (see Plate V., figs. 26 and 27, for the specimens of the first and second coins); but as the subject of the silver coinage of D. João V. is an extensive one, I reserve it for further consideration in the next and concluding paper of this series.

LAMINA V

21

22

23

24

25

26

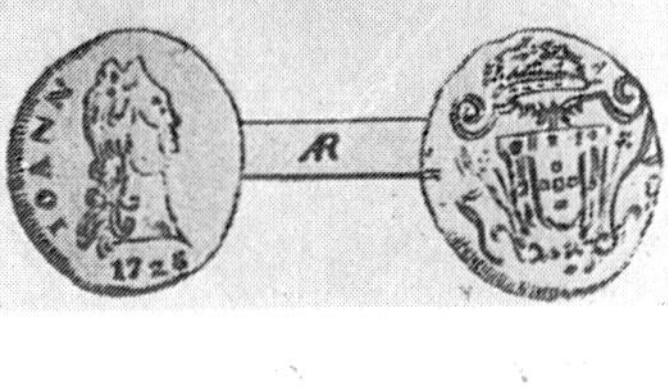

27

CONTRIBUTIONS

TO THE

STUDY OF INDO-PORTUGUESE NUMISMATICS.

BY

J. GERSON DA CUNHA,

M.R.C.S. AND L.M., ENG.; L.R.C.P., EDIN.;

Knight of the Order of St. Gregory the Great; Member of the Committee of Management of the Bombay Branch of the Royal Asiatic Society; Member of the Royal Asiatic Society of Great Britain and Ireland; Corresponding Member of the Royal Academy of Sciences of Lisbon; of the Oriental Academy of Florence; of the Academy of Science, Literature and Arts of Lyon; of the Arcadia of Rome; of the Adriatic Society of the Natural Sciences of Trieste; of the I.R. Zoological and Botanical Society of Vienna; Fellow of the Geographical Society of Italy, and of that of Lisbon; Fellow of the University of Bombay, &c.

FASCICULUS IV.

Bombay:

PRINTED AT THE

EDUCATION SOCIETY'S PRESS, BYCULLA

1880.

LÂMINA VI

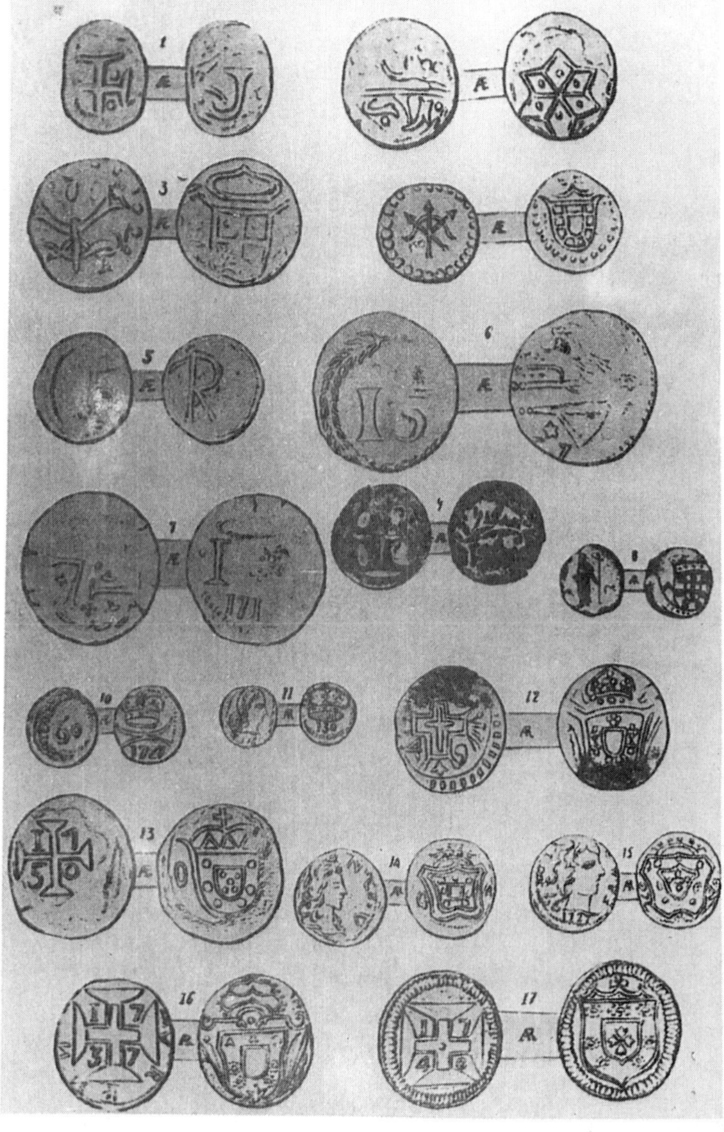

FASCICULUS IV.

The fourth and last part of this series of papers embraces the period from 1730 A.D. to the present time. The third part ended about the middle of the reign of King D. João V., which reign extended from 1706 to 1750; but as the coinage of this king consists of a large variety of types, I reserved some of them for consideration in this part.

The long interval that has elapsed since the presentation of the third paper, having, however, brought to light several obsolete specimens of inedited designs belonging to times before alluded to, I have been obliged to recede a step to describe them first, attributing them to their proper time and places in chronological sequence, and then resume the course thus interrupted. These frequent additions, often out of order, to the series of coins, indicate once again the many gaps that exist, and the chance one has still by persevering researches of filling them up.

To begin, then, with the coins appertaining to periods already referred to, we have, first of all, a copper piece appropriated to the time of the viceroyalty of D. João de Castro, from 1545 to 1548. This is the *bazarucco*, struck at the rate of 25 pardaos a quintal, whereby that viceroy reduced to the market value the abnormal rate of 36 pardaos ordered by his predecessor.

The specimen in my cabinet (see Plate VI., fig. 1,) is considerably worn out, clipped and slightly corroded, having been for years underground, as shown by its state of patination. It weighs now 65 grains Troy, the original weight was 168 Portuguese grains, the proportion between the two metrical systems being 5 Troy grains equal to 6 Portuguese ones. Mr. Aragão, in the appendix to his before-mentioned work,* says of this coin :—" To the Government of D. João de Castro, by the description given at page 138, ought to be attributed the following coin, which we obtained about fifteen days ago, and now belongs to the royal cabinet of Ajuda.

* *Descripção Geral e Historica das Moedas, &c.* Lisbon: 1880. Vol. iii., p. 607.

"Y. crowned, having on each side four points, and one in the centre. *Reverse.*—St. George's cross, having in each angle one point. Weight, 168 grains. Æ.—Inedited."

The author has illustrated this rare coin not only at the page where it is described, but also on the cover of his volume. My specimen was, doubtless, a duplicate of this one when in fine state of preservation. The find of a heap of these coins, mentioned in a book published only a couple of years ago, justifies once more the practice of the keepers of great national collections of coins not consenting to pay more than a fixed sum of money for examples supposed at the time to be unique, as a lot of them often turn up in the course of excavations, as in the present case. The notice of this find, and the description of the coins, although faulty in some respects, is given in the *Archæological Survey of Western India*, No. 10, thus:—"During the excavations in making a path round the contour of the great reservoir at Vihar, in Salsette, in January 1855, upwards of a thousand copper coins were dug up in an earthen pot. They were much corroded, but of some of the best of them drawings were made by the Messrs. West. As no notice has been published of these, it may not be uninteresting to have a reproduction of the drawings preserved, which is done in the accompanying plate. Three of them are distinctly Muhammadan, and not of a very early type. Only about half-a-dozen were of this coinage, and most of the others bear a cross on one side with a point between each of the arms; and on the obverse is a small figure like a Maltese cross with a point on each side of it, over which is a line bent down at each end, and the remainder of the field is occupied by a symbol—the intent of which is very doubtful—between two sets of four points. A sixth has a rude outline of a cross on one side of it, the other being plain. Other pieces of copper of similar sizes were quite smooth."* The figure in the plate of drawings above mentioned is placed in an inverted position, the result being that the crown is described as a Maltese cross having over it a line bent down at each end, and the letter Y as a symbol the intent of which is very doubtful. One other specimen, resembling somewhat the above described, is now in my cabinet. It seems to have been struck at Goa in the reign of D. Sebastião, and is attributable to the viceroyalty of D. Constantino da Bragança. It was picked up amongst the ruins of the old city of Bassein, not far from Bombay.

* Bombay, 1881, p. 66.

Obv.—Y crowned, with points and lines on each side.

Rev.—Three arrows crossing, a bow for each arrow. Copper. Weight, 66 grains Troy. Inedited. (Plate VI., fig. 2.)

King D. Sebastian succeeded to the throne of Portugal on the death of D. João III. in 1557. The bazarucco first described having the Y crowned, refers to D. João alone; while the second with the Y crowned on one side, and the arrows on the other, relates to both the kings, D. João and D. Sebastião, the Y to the former and the arrows to the latter, in memory of the martyrdom of the saint whose name he bore. It is clear, then, that this second bazarucco was issued soon after the death of King D. João. III.

With regard to the copper pieces with a sheaf of arrows on one side and the coat-of-arms on the other, I have already described and illustrated two specimens (see Plates II. and III., figs. 3 and 4 respectively). The first of these weighs 155 grains Troy, and the second 305 grains. Since then I have received four more specimens of the same type, of different sizes, and of corresponding difference in weight. It seems, indeed, that there was a graduated series of the bazaruccos of King D. Sebastião, which has but of late come to light. Of this latter series the largest weighs 130 grains Troy, and the smallest 80. (See Plate VI., figs. 3 and 4.)

A coin following the above in chronological order was described as belonging to either one or all of the three Filippes, who from 1580 to 1640 reigned in Portugal. (See Plate III., fig. 3.) It weighed 166 grains Troy, while a second specimen weighed only 125 grains. Of this type, also, a graduated series has of late been discovered, the smallest weighing only 80 grains Troy (see Plate VI., fig. 5), the largest being the one first described and drawn on the plate above-mentioned, viz.—Plate III., fig. 3.

Finally I have to refer to a coin already described. (See Plate II., fig. 5.) It is a copper piece, having on the obverse the value in reis, viz. 15, with a star above and below the number; and what on the reverse once resembled CCC. is now found to be the crown, having under it the figures I * V., *i. e.*, João V., with a star between them. In the exergue one can read the remains of the year 1717, when the piece was most probably struck at Bassein. (See Plate VI., fig. 6.) Weight, 222 grains Troy. Three specimens of this coin, more or less legible, are now in my cabinet, varying slightly in weight. Although no written document, hitherto known, refers to this kind of copper coinage, the initials of King D. João V., and the figures reading like 1717 in the exergue, appear to indicate the coin to have been struck during the reign of D. João, V. and issued from the Bassein mint, some years before the fall of that once famous "Court of the North" in 1739 into the hands of the Marâṭhâs.

Another coin, resembling the above in some respects, and most probably issued from the same mint, is also in my cabinet. It is inedited also, as far as I know.

Obv.—The number 7½ within an ill-defined circle with points on the left and below the number, representative of the value of the coin in reis.

Rev.—The initial ofKing D. João V. under the crown, the next figure, which ought to have been V., being badly struck. The year 1711 in the exergue. Copper. Weight, 115 grains Troy. (See Plate VI., fig. 7.)

This coin is evidently the half of the one last described.

Having now completed the description of the copper coins, hitherto inedited, belonging to former times, or not all embraced by the period to which the present paper refers, I pass on to describe the two following silver coins:—

Obv.—The coat-of-arms of the kingdom with the mint mark G-A (*i. e.*, Goa,) on the margin.

Rev.—The cross of the Order of Christ, with the year 1593 in the angles. Billon. Weight, 80 grains Troy. (See Plate VI., fig. 8.)

Obv.—The figure of St. Philip standing to the left, with a long staff or cross in the right hand, between the letters M and A, the mint mark of Malacca. The date in the exergue is now invisible.

Rev.—The coat-of-arms of the kingdom between the letters G and A. Silver. Weight, grains Troy 28¾. (See Plate VI., fig. 9.)

As all the coins are represented of the exact size, I abstain from declaring their diameter in millimètres or in inches and tenths.

The former of these coins is difficult of appropriation to any viceroy with even a tolerable amount of certainty. It all depends upon the correct reading of the date, which is far from distinct. If 1593, the coin must be the silver *meio xerafim* of the Governor Manuel de Sousa Coutinho, who decreed the issue of such a coin with a considerable amount of alloy, and it may have continued to be struck during the viceroyalty of his successor, Mathias d'Albuquerque. Manuel de Sousa

Coutinho, whose rule ended in 1591, ordered the issue of the silver xerafins only, with its sub-divisions; while Mathias d' Albuquerque, who governed from the latter date to 1597, commanded the coining of money in four metals. Whether among the latter the xerafim of base silver or billon is to be included no document exists to inform us. If the year, instead of 1593, be read 1693, then the coin must be the *meio xerafim*, struck in the reign of D. Pedro II., and during the governorship of a triple provisional commission on the death of the Governor D. Miguel d'Almeida. In that case this coin was issued in accordance with the regulations dated 1681, bearing on one side the coat-of-arms of the kingdom between the mint mark G—A, and the cross of the Order of Christ with the year in its angles on the other.

The second coin is most probably the silver *meia tanga*, said in official papers of the time to have been ordered by the Viceroy Conde de Linhares to be struck at Goa early in 1631, when sending pecuniary help to Malacca, then threatened by the Dutch. The letters M—A on the obverse evidently refer to this fact. It is true that no exergual date is visible; but coins of this type, excepting the letters M—A, they being issued for circulation only in India, exist, bearing the year 1640, perhaps the last issue of that type. The effigy of St. Philip is impressed in honour of the reigning sovereign, D. Filippe III. of Portugal and IV. of Spain. It was often the custom among peninsular people of those days of ostentatious piety, to impress the figure of the saint of the king's name instead of his own portrait.

I have already explained the origin and meanings of the terms *xerafim* and *tanga*; but I have also lately seen somewhere that the kings of Persia used to coin their money at a place called Ashraf, from which mint city the *ashrafi* may have derived its name, so being originally the name of a Persian coin it was subsequently applied to two kinds of Indian coinage, in the same way as the monetary names Venitian and Florin are derived from coins struck in Venice and Florence.

To pass on now to describe in chronological sequence the issues of money in Portuguese India from 1730, I must begin with the subdivisions of the rupia of D. João V., already described and illustrated along with the pardao or meia rupia, at the end of Part III. (See Plate V., figs. 26 and 27.)

The sub-divisions of the rupee of D. João V. were *pardao*, or half-a-rupee, *meio pardao*, or quarter-rupee, *tánga* or one-tenth, and *meia tanga*, one-twentieth of a rupee.

We first meet with the word *rupia* in Portuguese Numismatics in an official document dated the 21st of November 1668, not, however, as a denomination of any Portuguese coin, but as that of a foreign one, enumerated along with Persian *abasis*, *sadis*, *apáras*, to which may be added *patacas* or Spanish dollars, and silver in plate and bar, all to be changed into *xerafins* of Goa, in accordance with the resolution dated the 18th February 1650. All this silver in coin and bullion was captured from an Arab fleet by D. Jeronymo Manuel.*

Two years before, *i. e.* in 1666, a silver coin, called *xerafim dobrado* (double xerafim) was struck during the viceroyalty of Conde d'Alvor.† This coin was some time later called *rupia*, a designation that has been preserved to the present day ; while the words *xerafim* and *pardao* have become synonymous. The inscription of the word *rupia* on the coin, however, began later still, not before the beginning of the reign of King D. José, from 1755.

The use or employment of the word rupia or rupee in the annals of Indian coinage in general is of a comparatively modern date. The early Muhammadan rulers used the Arabic designations of dinar, dirhem and falus for the gold, silver and copper coins respectively, words belonging originally to the Greek, Roman and Byzantine systems, until the Pathán Sultans introduced the word tankás for both their gold and silver coinage. Shir-Shah, of the family of Sur, was the first to introduce the word *rupia* in substitution of the silver tanka between the years 1540 and 1545, a designation which was soon adopted by the Moghul Emperors, by the Portuguese, and the East India Company.‡

The origin of the word rupee has been traced to two sources, viz., Sanskrit *rûpa*, meaning 'figure,' 'image,' and *rúpyam*, which means

---

* Aragão, *ut supra*, pp. 253 and 546.

† *Ibid.*, *p.* 264.

‡ Abul Fazel bears witness to the fact of the word rupiah (روپیه) not being in use before the reign of Shir-Shah. He writes :—" Rupiah is a silver coin of a round form, in weight 11¼ *mashas*. It was first introduced in the time of Shir-Shah, and under the present reign (that of Akbar) it has been revised and made more pure." The *Ain Akbari* seems to relate to the year 963 A. H., 1556 of our era.

'silver.' Pâṇini uses the word *rûpya* in the sense of 'struck,' derived from *rûpa* 'form,' 'shape,' &c. (See Vopa-deva. xxii., 2.) The latter origin, *i.e.*, that of *rûpyam* or 'silver,' appears to be the correct one, as no Muhammadan prince would allow any effigy or figure to be impressed on his coinage, with one or two exceptions well known to students of Numismatics. This derivation bears out, also, the argument of analogy from an ancient source. The Greeks, for instance, employed among themselves the generical term 'silver' for money; in like manner the chief silver coin of India has now for more than three centuries received its name from *rûpyam*, or modern vernacular *rupem*, 'silver,' just as the ancient Greek idea of expressing a solemn compact by means of sealing, or placing the stamp or seal upon a piece of metal, guaranteeing the exactness of its weight and purity of the metal, has its counterpart in the Indian *mohur*, a Persian word, originally meaning 'a seal.'

Some of the foreign writers of the seventeenth and eighteenth century, when describing the Indian coinage, especially of the Moghul Empire, often mention the gold and silver rupees of India, and the East India Company had, not long ago, a gold rupee current in this Presidency. The meaning to be attached to the phrase 'gold rupee' ought evidently to be the value of the gold coin in silver; for, literally speaking, it comes to mean simply 'gold silver coin,' which is absurd.

Mr. E. Thomas, an eminent authority on Oriental Numismatics, says that the origin of the Indian rupee, not with reference to its name, but as far as its weight is concerned, "may be traced up to the very early times, in the Âryan *Sataraktika* or Sátakrishnala, the *even* one hundred *rati* weight, which formed the basis of the standard gold and silver pieces of the early Páthan kings of Delhi (A. D. 1228), each of which weighed 100 ratis, or 175 grains, and were conventionally termed *Tankas*."*

Of the reign of D. João V., I will now describe the issues of money and the alterations made from time to time, under each of his viceroys, illustrating only the typical specimens of each period, and omitting the sub-divisions or fractions of monetary units, which details one may well dispense with unless these fractions bear a different design.

---

* The *Indian Antiquary*, Bombay, 1882, Vol. XI., p. 318.

D. Rodrigo da Costa.

Viceroy of India from 1707 *to* 1712.

During the viceroyalty of D. Rodrigo da Costa it was resolved on the 12th of August 1710 that a mark of silver in dollars should have the value fixed at 30 xerafins, individuals carrying to the mint a mark in dollars receiving in exchange 30 xerafins, 1 tanga, and 15 reis. At this rate a xerafim weighed 153 Portuguese grains.

Vasco Fernandes Cesar de Menezes.

From 1712 *to* 1717.

In 1713 this viceroy determined, by his decree of the 9th of September, that private persons should receive from the mint for each mark of gold, of the kind known as *pão da China* of 23 carats, 96 *S. Thomés* of 56½ grs. each, of the value of 5 xerafins, while the old *S. Thomés*, weighing 68 grs., should circulate for 6 xerafins and 15 reis. This gave origin to the denomination of *novos* and *velhos S. Thomés*, the old ones being those struck before 1713. The excess of 816 grains in the China gold was due to the coined gold being reduced to 18 carats, and the object of the decree was to facilitate the issue of colonial money, which was getting scarce.

In 1716 it was resolved that the tutenag coinage, called *bazaruccos*, should contain one-fourth of tin, such an amalgam rendering the falsification of the coin more difficult.

The above viceroy was succeeded by the Archbishop D. Sebastião de Andrade Pessanha, pending the arrival of the viceroy. During his rule, from 16th January to 16th October 1717, no alteration was made in the monetary affairs of Portuguese India. He was followed by the Viceroy Conde da Ericeira, from 1717 to 1720. During this time the only mint regulation published was that the coins of 10 bazaruccos should weigh 369 grains, and its fractions proportionately.

Francisco José de Sampaio e Castro.

1720—1723.

During this period a silver rupee of the type already illustrated was issued. (See Plate V., fig. 26.) Also the tutenag series of coins, viz., 10, 7½, 5, and 2½ bazaruccos, some of which have been represented at the same plate. This viceroy was succeeded by D. Christovão de Mello only for two months, and then by a commission presided over by the Archbishop D. Ignacio de Santa Thereza, from 1723 to 1725. All this time no change appears to have been recorded in the numismatic annals of Portuguese India.

João de Saldanha da Gama.

1725—1732.

In 1726 it was resolved that rupees and their fractions, viz., pardao, meio pardao, tanga, and meia tanga should be issued. Specimens of this coinage, although very rare, are extant. The first three are of the type already illustrated. The type, however, often varied at short intervals in obedience to the whim or at the dictation of the officers of the mint, as will be shown more at length hereafter. The *tanga* and *meia tanga* of this period bear designs entirely distinct from the three coins above mentioned.

Obv.—Two palm leaves joined, the royal crown above, the date 1727 beneath.

Rev.—A laurel crown with 60, representing the value in *reis*, in the centre. Silver. *Tanga*. Weight, 16 grains Troy. (See Plate VI., fig. 10.)

Obv.—The laureate bust of the king to the right between two palms. 1750 in the exergue.

Rev.—30, indicative of the value in *reis*, the royal crown above. Silver. *Meia tanga*. Weight, 10 grains Troy. (See Plate VI., fig. 11.) Both the specimens are in my collection.

There are three other types of the *tanga*, viz.—the bust of the king, name round the margin, and date below on the obverse, and 60 beneath the royal crown on the reverse;—bust and date without a legend on the obverse, and 60 under the royal crown on the reverse; and lastly, the cross of the Order of Christ with the date in its angles on the obverse, and the coat-of-arms of the kingdom on the reverse.

Of the *meia tanga* there is one other design, that of two palms united about the middle, the royal crown above, the year below, on the obverse, and the numeral 30, indicative of its value, within a circle of *grénetis* on the reverse. Mr. Aragão describes, at p. 290 of his work, a *meio pardao*, struck during this viceroyalty, weighing 52 Portuguese grains, and bearing the design similar to the *tanga* last mentioned. At Diu, the coinage of this period bore the following type :—Coat-of-arms of the kingdom between the letter D—O, the mint mark of Diu, on the obverse ; and the cross of St. Thomas in the field, with the year in the angles, on the reverse.

The only gold coin issued during this viceroyalty was the S. Thomé, bearing, on one side, the coat-of-arms of the kingdom, and the cross of that Saint with 12 and X, indicative of the value of the coin in 12 xerafins, in the two upper angles, and the date in the lower ones, on the other.

The Provisional Commission, which governed from January to November 1732, did not alter the coinage as was established in Goa and other Settlements by former governors. It was followed by

D. Pedro Mascarenhas.

From 1732 *to* 1741.

During this time gold and silver coins were issued, gold and silver from the Goa mint, and silver alone from that of Diu. The silver coinage of Goa did not differ in type from the one above described; the gold one, however, which is illustrated by Mr. Aragão at p. 296, from a unique example, bears on the obverse the legend IH. CR. V. S. P. S. (*IHesus ChRistus Venit Salvare Populum Suum*) round the margin, the cross of St. Thomas in the middle, having the date 1737 in the lower angles; while the reverse has the usual coat-of-arms of the kingdom. It weighs 112 Portuguese grains.

This viceroy ordered the coining of 30,000 xerafins in silver into *cruzados* and their fractions at Goa for circulation at Mozambique. His successor, D. Luiz de Menezes, from 1741 to 1742, continued the issue of money as before. He appointed a committee of four learned financiers to report upon the causes of the depreciation of the *bazaruccos* in the market, and to indicate means to remedy the evil. They sent in a report replete with Latin quotations, but did not come to any practical conclusion. When economists and Latinists as these work to so poor a result, one may infer that the whole thing, from beginning to end, was *une affaire flambée*, not unlike many of the transactions of that Government.

This viceroy was followed by another Provisional Commission, who governed from 1742 to 1744, and while almost continuously fighting against the Marâṭhâs, had time enough to attend to the affairs of the mint, from which issued money in gold, silver, and tutenag. The coining of the latter metal or alloy into *rodas* caused considerable trouble in adjusting and readjusting their value to that of *reis*. They not only issued the *rodas* already described and illustrated, but fixed the proportion to *reis* and *bazaruccos* as follows:— 1 roda = $1\frac{1}{4}$ reis = $1\frac{2}{3}$ bazaruccos.

The average price of tin was then 55 xerafins the quintal, which, deducting the expenses of refining the metal, left the balance of 28 xerafins for the coiners to pay the cost of mintage and the seignorage.

D. Pedro Miguel de Almeida Portugal,

From 1744 *to* 1750.

During this viceroyalty coins in gold, silver, copper and tutenag were issued both from the Goa and Diu mints. The Goa coinage of the period does not differ from that of the former viceroyalties, the golden *S. Thomés* bearing the cross of the Saint on one side and the coat-of-arms of the kingdom on the other ; while the silver coinage consisted of the *rupia* and its sub-divisions of the type above described. From the Diu mint were issued rupees and their halves, copper *atiás* and tutenag *bazaruccos*. The latter two kinds of money will be frequently mentioned hereafter, and their type was for years of an immutable character, which was not the case with the rupee of this period. Its type was peculiar to the time, and has never since then been once repeated.

Obv.—St. George's cross, ornamented, having the figures of the year 1749 in its four angles.

Rev.—The coat-of-arms of the kingdom. Silver. *Rupia* of Diu. Weight, 145 grains Troy. (See Plate VI., fig. 12.) In my collection. For nearly a decade, it seems, this design was used for the silver coinage of Diu. It resembles somewhat the silver coinage struck at Goa in the reign of D. Pedro II., and the viceroyalty of Francisco de Tavora, from 1681 to 1686. For the resemblance the two rupees bear to each other, although issued at the distance of more than half a century, see Plate IV., fig. 19. The *meia rupia* of Diu, bearing the same design and the year 1749, and weighing 43 grains Troy, is also in my collection. Both the above coins were sent to me from Diu by Mr. L. L. Flores, Advocate General in that old Portuguese Settlement. Of the copper pieces struck at Diu, the following example, out of a large number of specimens, bearing diverse dates, will be sufficient :—

Obv.—Cross of the Order of Christ with the date 1750 in its angles.

Rev.—The coat-of-arms of the kingdom between the letters D—O, the mint mark of Diu. Copper. *Atiá.* Weight, 140 grains Troy. (See Plate VI., fig. 13.)

Of the tutenag coinage I have already described some examples, and given a photograph at Plate I., fig. 7.

The year 1750 not only closes the reign of D. João V., but *also* the most uncertain, vacillating period of the numismatic history of Portuguese India. All those persons who have devoted their time and attention to the study of colonial numismatology of the Portuguese—and their number is unfortunately very limited—have found the subject extremely difficult. One must be groping in the dark, getting light only when, in the absence of genuine specimens, positive data can be patiently extracted from written records preserved in the archives of the Government at the metropolis or in the colonies, or when amongst the ruins of their once numerous settlements one can be so fortunate as to meet with the extremely rare chance of making discoveries of hoards or *trouvaille*. It is only from the end of the reign of D. João V. that one can steer clear from amidst a multitude of numismatic documents in four metals, all, unlike the early coins, dated and bearing perceptible legends. In fact we have hitherto had paucity of materials and scarcity of examples, supplemented as they were by written official documents. Now there is abundance of both, and the difficulty lies in what to choose and what to reject, in order to ensure a methodical arrangement of the subject. All coins, however, both early and late, are remarkable alike for the rudeness of execution and barbarous shape of the characters stamped upon them.

The coins of D. João V., struck at the beginning of his reign, are not only rare, but many of them bear types suggested entirely by the fancy of the minters, without any sanction from a higher authority, or guarantee based on similar designs at home or amongst the neighbouring native princes. The coinage from 1750 onwards was all this time current in the country, until the Monetary Convention of the Anglo-Portuguese treaty caused it entirely to cease to pass as circulating medium since a couple of years ago, and is now so very scarce as to be found only in the trays of collectors of coins.

The monetary nomenclature of the Portuguese in India has, with the exception of the first issues from Albuquerque and his early successors, who had *manues*, *espheras*, *S. Thomés* and *patacões*, been derived from a wholly Oriental source, viz.:—*xerafim*, (Persian), *pardao*, *tanga*, *rupia*, (Indian), *bazaruccos*, (Perso-Indian), *rub* or quarter of a *tanga*, (Arabic). But in the matter of designs they have, contrary to the habit of the English, French, Dutch and Danes, always abstained from imitating native prototypes, and from inscribing any Indian character.

In the matter of types, then, the Portuguese coins at home have always furnished the prototypes, being mostly crosses of several heraldic orders, such as of Christ, St. Benedict of Aviz, St. George, besides the Christian symbols of the cross of St. Thomas, the arrows of St. Sebastian, and the wheel of St. Catherine—struck exclusively for India in general, and Goa in particular;—the figures of the patron saints, instead of their own portraits, of the kings bearing the names of Sebastian, Philip, and John; and finally the everlasting coat-of-arms of the kingdom.

Even the legends relating to the name and title of reigning sovereigns were more or less similar, as they ought to have been, to those on the coins of Portugal, as was also almost necessarily the usual royal crown. And in one instance, during the reign of D. Filippe II., the silver coin had inscribed round the margin the old Christian legend of *In hoc signo vinces.*

It was in the reign of D. Manuel "the Fortunate," from 1495 to 1521, that this motto first made its appearance in Portugal, but it was not introduced into India until a century later, during the reign of D. Fillippe II. of Portugal and III. of Spain. A coin of D. Manuel, now in the collection of His Majesty King D. Luis I. of Portugal, has on the obverse the following legend:—*Primus Emanuel R. Portugaliæ Alg. Citra Ultra in Africa Dominus Guinee, In Commercii, Navigatione Æthiopiæ, Arabiæ, Persiæ India,* and on the reverse:—*In Hoc Signo Vinces.** This coin was issued soon after the discovery of India, by the route of the Cape of Good Hope, by the Admiral Vasco da Gama, and commemorates two important facts, viz.:—The discovery itself and the subjection of both Africa and Asia in spiritual matters to the Priory Major of the Order of Christ, attached to the Vicariate of Thomar, by the Bull *pro excellenti* of Pope Leo X.

The lordship or dominion of the conquests of Africa and Asia, and the subsequent nomination of one of his subjects to the spiritual supremacy of the Christianity of the two continents, naturally made D. Manuel "the Fortunate" persuade himself that he was entitled to have inscribed on his coins the motto of the first Christian Roman Emperor, which his successors almost steadily continued to claim as their inheritance.

---

* *Memoria das Moedas Cunhadas em Portugal*; por M. B. Lopes Fernandes. Lisbon: 1856. Vol. i., p. 113.

Apropos of this legend on the Indo-Portuguese coin, one does not know what amount of credit to attach to the tale or tradition about the origin of the motto, but it runs thus:—Constantine, determined to stop the tyranny of Maxentius, who had possession of Italy, judged it to be folly to worship those who were not gods, and thought it incumbent on him to honour the god of his father Constantine, surnamed Chlorus, "the Pale," one of the two Cæsars, appointed by Maximilian and Diocletian, who died at Eboracum (York) in Britain, on an expedition against the Picts in July 306. Having some Christian principles, Constantine is said to have prayed, and, while praying, seen about midday the luminous trophy of the cross in the sky, with the inscription "In hoc signo vinces." The army are said to have witnessed it. But Constantine, doubting the import of the apparition, continued to meditate on it till night, which was the night before the last and decisive battle with Maxentius at the village of Saxa Rubra near Rome. During sleep Christ appeared with the sign he had seen in the heavens, and commanded him to make a standard resembling the sign, and to use it as a safeguard against his enemies. He then ordered the shields of his soldiers to be inscribed with the figure of the sacred monogram of the name of Christ, and the same device to be worked in gold and precious stones on his own standard, or *labarum* (from Bretagnic *lab* 'to raise' or Basque *labarva* 'standard' or '*labor*'). With this he advanced against Maxentius, defeated him, and Constantine became the sole master of the West.*

He had now his mind turned to the East, and what the Great Alighieri says regarding this, of Constantine 'the Great'—

> Posciachè Costantin l' aquila volse
> Contra il corso del ciel, ch'ella seguio
> Dietro all' antico che Lavinia tolse,
>
> (Paradiso, c. 6, v. 1-3.)

may one fairly apply, with respect at least to the tendency of his policy, to D. Manuel 'the Fortunate' and his successors. There is this difference however, that whatever may have been the motives of Constantine in his encouragement of the propagation of Christianity, and in his love of the East, D. Manuel was truly sincere, the copying of Constantine's motto on his coins being but the outcome of his deep faith in Christianity, a faith, moveover, raised to that pitch of

* Cf. Eusebius, *Vit. Const.* i., c. 28-29.

fanaticism which embodied the genuine religious spirit of the times in which he lived.

I have alluded above to the capricious manner in which the moneyers in Goa changed the type of coins, not only during the same reign, but also and often during one short viceroyalty or governorship. In elucidation of this fact are adduced below the description and illustration of some of the unpublished designs during the reign of D. João V.

Obv.—Laureled bust of the king to the right, dividing the legend P.ET.A.R.—IOA.V. (Portugaliæ et Algarbiorum Rex—Joannes V.) In the exergue the year 1709.

Rev.—The coat-of-arms of the kingdom. Silver. *Pardao*. In the collection of Mr. J. M. do Carmo Nazareth, of Pangim. Weight, unknown.

Obv.—Laureled bust of the king to the right, dividing the legend IOAN—NES. V. Date illegible.

Rev.—The coat-of-arms of the kingdom, having on the sides G-A. (Goa). Silver. *Meio pardao*. Weight, 43 grains Troy. In my collection. (See Plate VI., fig. 14.)

Obv.—Bust as above—IOANNE—S. V. R. P. (Joannes V., Rex. Portugaliæ). In the exergue the year 1727.

Rev.—The coat-of-arms of the kingdom, having on the left 150, the value of the coin in *reis*, and G.A. (Goa) on the right. Silver. *Meio pardao*. Weight, 43 grains Troy. In my collection also. (See Plate VI., fig. 15.)

There are multiples also of the two coins last described in one or two collections; but the examples given above are representative of the series.

The late Felippe Neri Xavier, whose little *Memoria*, before referred to, although incomplete, is an aid to the study of Indo-Portuguese coins, affording valuable information, especially for the later years of the Portuguese rule in India, regarding the fineness, weight, type and changes in the value of coins hitherto issued, states that he once saw a rupee bearing on one side the coat-of-arms of the kingdom with the mint mark G—A., and the cross of the Order of Christ with the year 1735 in its angles, and the legend Joannes V. R. P. on the other.* Weight, as given by the writer, is 3 drachms and 19 Portuguese grains.

* P. 87.

Now this coin and the two following, belonging to the cabinet of the Bombay Branch of the Royal Asiatic Society, show plainly how the short interval of six years, included in the viceroyalty of Conde de Sandomil, who ruled in India from 1732 to 1741, was fruitful among the master-coiners of Goa in the issue of three different types. Those of the B. B. Royal Asiatic Society are as follows :—

Obv.—The cross of the Order of Christ in the field with the year 1737 in its angles. The legend round the margin is indistinct, the character NNE—V.R.P only being visible, and these stamped in a manner different from that of the other coins.

Rev.—The coat-of-arms of the kingdom. Silver. *Rupia.* Weight, 180 grains Troy. (See Plate VI., fig. 16.)

Obv.—The cross of the Order of Christ as above, with the year 1740. No legend, except V., close to the right arm of the cross. The whole within a beaded circle.

Rev.—The coat-of-arms of the kingdom, differently impressed from the above. Silver. *Rupia.* Weight, 185 grains Troy. (See Plate VI., fig. 17.)

It is indeed almost phenomenal in the history of coinages of the world to see so rapid and so repeated alterations in the types of money. Another circumstance not less remarkable in the currency of Portuguese India, was the haste with which the old designs were withdrawn from circulation the moment a new one was introduced. The foreign travellers, Italian, French, English, and Dutch, who visited Goa during the XVIth and XVIIth centuries, and whose most important statements relating to the subject I have already quoted, appear, however, to have been struck by the multiplicity of types, some of which must have been concurrent. It is strange, for instance, to hear Jean-Albert de Mandelslo, ambassador of the Duke of Holstein, who visited Goa in January 1639, informing us that he saw at Goa at that time coins of the reign of D. Sebastian, viz., 1557—1578, which were in circulation. However, as his reference to the Goa currency is an interesting one, and his authority, perhaps, not less trustworthy than that of other travellers, here is what he says :—" In Goa there are various kinds of coins, the smallest of which are the *bazarucques,* with a sphere on one, and two arrows crossing each other on the other side; they are made of a metal formed of pewter and tin mixed together. Eight of these *bazarucques* make one *vintem,*

5 of which make one *tanghè*, and 5 *tanghes* one silver *serafin*, which is according to a royal order worth 300 *reis*, and six *tanghes* make one *pardai*. The *serafin* has on one side the effigy of St. Sebastian and on the other a bundle of arrows. There are also golden *serafins*, formerly coined at Ormus, but of so high a value that it is not approached by that of any other Indian coin, wherefore also the goldsmiths work up in their business all those which fall into their hands. They have also *Santomes* of 16 *tanghes*, and *pagodas* of 14, 15, and 16 *tanghes*. Foreign merchants entering the town, pay 8 per cent. on all wares, and as much when they depart, but the custom house revenue farmers are so reasonable in their estimates of the goods, that the merchants have not much occasion to complain on this subject. They also observe a rule, that when a merchant has paid entrance dues and does not sell all his goods, he may carry them away without paying export dues, so that likewise a foreign merchant who has bought spices or other goods of Malacca, or of China, from a Portuguese, a citizen of Goa, may charge them to the name of the vendor, and exempt himself by this means from paying the export dues."*

The *bazarucques* of the writer who describes them as "made of a metal formed of pewter and tin mixed together" are the tutenag and tin *bazaruccos* first coined by the Portuguese at Goa. The question of the introduction and coinage of this amalgam has already been discussed. Further inquiries into the matter have, however, forced the conviction that this kind of low and debased currency was first noticed by the Portuguese at Malacca, where, and in the whole of the Malay Peninsula, perhaps also in the adjacent islands of the Archipelago, this amalgam was used for the purpose of coinage, from time immemorial, under their native princes.† The Portuguese, observing its usefulness in their new settlement of Malacca, gradually introduced it into Western India, and also into Eastern Africa, giving it the generic name of *bazaruccos*, which the English, in their new Dependency of Bombay, changed into *budgrooks*; but of this more hereafter.

The Portuguese called these tutenag and tin coins *bazaruccos* generally, the design on them was a cross of one pattern or another on one side, and the coat-of-arms of the kingdom on the other. But then out

* See p. 259 of the Amsterdam Edition in French of Jean-Albert de Mandelslo's Travels. In this work reference is also made to the Gujarât currency.

† Cf. "Tin-money in the trading ports of the Burman Empire," in *The Numismatic Chronicle*, Vol. VII., pp. 27, *et seq.* Lond. 1844-45.

of the same alloy they struck another kind of a serial coinage, which bore on the obverse a wheel, and this coin with its sub-divisions went by the name of 'roda.' I have already referred to this coin, and explained its origin as having been issued in honour of St. Catherine, virgin and martyr, the patron Saint of Goa.

The 'roda' was symbolical of the conquest or recapture of Goa by the Portuguese on the 25th of November 1510, the day consecrated in the Christian calendar to St. Catherine of Alexandria, who is said to have been broken upon a wheel under Maximianus, *circa* 306 A. D.

In heraldry her wheel has 8 spokes, and a corresponding number of hook-like iron spikes, on the outer side. The wheel of the coins does not count so many spokes, but on the arms of the Senate or Municipal Chamber of Goa, and of its Metropolitan See, of both of which ancient civic and ecclesiastical institutions of the city it constitutes a leading emblem in their respective coats, it does plainly exhibit that number. As an illustration of the fact I append below a facsimile of the oval seal of the Metropolitan Chapter of the See of Goa, which bears round the wheel the following legend, beginning, next to a cross of the Order of Christ:—CAPIT. METROP. GOANVM, and closing with another cross of the same kind. The devotion to this saint and her feast day are of traditional importance and magnificence. The Government and the people vie with each other in celebrating the 25th of November with great solemnity. The national epic poet has not forgotten to duly commemorate the eventful day, saying:—

" Irão soldados inclytos fazendo
Mais que leões famelicos e touros
Na luz que sempre celebrada e dina
Será da Egypcia Sancta Catharina."*

O Lusiadas, C. X. e st. XLIII.

---

* This beautiful verse has been translated into English thus:—

" His gallant *soldiers* in more blood shall wade
Then *Lyons* pin'd, *Bulls* prickt with love and Ire;
Upon the *Feast* (as pat as by designe)
Of Egypt's *Virgin Martyr*, Katherine."

Fanshaw.

" His inclyt sold'iery more of fury shows
than rampant Bulls, or Lyons hunger-bold,
that Day for ever celebrate and digne
of Egypt's Martyr-maid, Saint Catherine."

Burton.

Both the translations are perfectly correct, and yet how different.

Besides Camões, the *Roman Breviary* contains, in honour of the patron saint of Goa, two hymns in Latin, said to have been composed by the *Congregados*, a religious association of Brâhmaṇ priests, members of distinguished families in Goa, who giving up their faith in Brâhmaṇ-ism, did not pledge themselves to abandon the privileges of their high caste. The *Congregados*, priests of the religious order of St. Philip Nery, and the *Theatins*, of that of St. Cajetanus of Theana, both of the Brâhmaṇ caste, were missionaries in Southern India and in Ceylon, where they made a considerable number of conversions to the Roman Catholic Church.*

These Nerysts wrote two hymns in honour of St. Catherine, which begin thus:—

(1) "Claram trophæis virginem,
Urbis Goensis præsidem,
Trino decoram stemmate
Laudemus omnes principem.

(2) "Virginis magnæ triplici corona
Sanguinis claræ sophiæ pudoris,
Quam dedit Nili Pharos alta, palmas,
Pangimus ore."

The second hymn ends in the following manner:—

"Laus Deo, virtus, decus ac potestas,
Qui Goæ tale mtribuit patronam,
Taleque auroræ jubar et refulgens,
Sidus olympo."

Brev. Roman. Olissiponi, 1876, O. P. D., pp. 2 and 4.

These curious Latin compositions of the Goa Brâhmaṇ missionaries will, doubtless, be a novelty to Orientalists; but they show how often insignificant coins and their not seldom apparently unmeaning impressions have attached to them some interesting historical facts. The verses may not perhaps merit the approval of critics, and I have heard it stated that in Rome the hymns were said to have been written in the "Asiatic" style.

But to return once more to the *bazaruccos*, the remarkably long reign of D. João V. was fruitful of complaints and trouble regarding

* Regarding the vital question of Christianity in India, in a review of Mr. Kaye's work (1860), it is remarked that the Rev. Mr. Long had urged strongly the necessity for native missionaries. The Calcutta reviewer writes:—"We believe that if Christianity is ever to take hold on the people of India it will be by native agency." The above case is in favour of this assertion.

the fluctuating character of the value of this low ready money. Although the care and charge of coining was everywhere entrusted to the kings, or their representatives and delegates, the royal prerogative was often not jealously guarded. Goldsmiths, dealers in bullion, *chitin*, (merchants) were authorized by prescriptive right to fabricate money, subject of course to control on the part of the governing power. This right of coining then was in Goa vested in particular individuals or farmers, who strove hard to keep the monopoly as long as they could, and make it within that time as lucrative as possible.

The evil was begun long before this period, the most notable instance being in 1687, during the first governorship of D Rodrigo da Costa, when it was resolved that one *bazarucco* should go to its half, *i. e.*, should suffer in exchange the loss of 50 per cent. To add to the complaint of the trader, who was defrauded by the deterioration of the former standard, a lot of the *bazaruccos* struck at Goa and sent to Mozambique and Mombaça to circulate there, had been returned as unnecessary. But to make matters worse, this very low money often became scarce, when the value of the metal not only rose above that of the metal coined,—for it could never descend below that of the metal sold by weight as mere bullion,—but, not unlike the precious metals, became one of the measures of value, being for a time less subject to variation. This was certainly one of those paradoxes to be met with only in the extremely faulty financial system of the Portuguese in India.

There must have been, however, some reasons to induce the much more practical and far-seeing English people to adopt the tutenag and tin coinage in their new Dependency of Bombay. It seems that it was an aim of the English in India to assimilate their issues of money as closely as possible to those of their neighbours in diverse parts of the country ; for many different coinages were current in India, whilst currencies of different provinces were of unequal values, hence arose the office of shroffage. The English in the early days of Bombay imitated the Portuguese currency, most probably to meet the facilities of commerce. Bruce tells us that the coinage of money was commenced on its own account by the East India Company in Bombay, which was held in independence. In 1671 the Court of Directors gave instructions to have a mint established upon the island, and a few years afterwards the measure was sanctioned by the Crown. A clause in the Charter, granted on the 26th year of the reign of Charles II., dated the 5th of October 1677, empowers the E. I. Company to coin money at Bombay, to be current wherever the privilege of trade in the East Indies extended, to be called by the name of rupees, pices and budgrooks, and that such money should not resemble British money.*

There was, it is true, no need for the English to go far to find a precedent for the issue of a tin coinage, when they had it at home. Coins were struck in tin in Ireland as well as in England. The English coinage of James II. of half-pence and farthings was in this metal. There was also tin coinage of Charles II., which was not extended to Ireland, and tin coins were issued for Ireland by William and Mary.†

But in Bombay the existence of similar coinage in the surrounding territory, which was then in the possession of the Portuguese, must have suggested their issue, which should be current not only "in the island, but in all the dependencies of the Company in the East Indies," which in the time referred to were, indeed, very limited.

Tavernier, whom I have already quoted elsewhere, says ;—"Since the present King of England married the Princess of Portugal, who had in part of her portion the famous port of Bombeye, where the English are very hard at work to build a strong fort, they coin both silver, copper and tin. But that money will not go to Surat......only it passes among the English in their fort, and some 2 or 3 leagues up in the country, and in the villages along the coast."‡ From this statement of Tavernier, Mr. Thomas, the eminent Oriental Numismatologist, concludes—"It would seem that the Portuguese and Dutch had already introduced a system of imitating the native currencies."§ Of the Dutch system of coining money I have not yet completed my studies, and consequently abstain from giving an opinion ; but as far as the Portuguese are concerned, I am quite certain that they never once from the day they first rounded the Cape of Good Hope to the present, imitated any kind of native currency, which was moreover against the Christian principles animating their governmental policy. What they did was simply to allow native coins, shroff-marked, denoting their genuineness in weight and touch, to circulate in their settlements at full value—a necessity of the trade relations with the natives of the country—and also to adopt some of the Eastern names of coins for their own coinage,

* Annals of the East India Company, II. 278. Also, Cæsar Moreau's East India Company's Records. Lond. 1825, p. 3.

† See the *Numismatic Chronicle*, New Series. Lond. 1863. Vol. III., p. 9.

‡ *Opus cit.*, p. 141.

§ The *Indian Antiquary*, Bombay. 1882. Vol. XI., p. 318.

as I have already said. Tavernier himself writes:—"Portugals had got beyond mere local issues and coined fine gold, with European devices, for the dependencies of Goa."* Then in the same place Mr. Thomas takes *pardaos* to be *patacas*. *Patacas* were and are still dollars; what *pardao* is I have fully explained elsewhere in one or more of the numbers of this series.

With regard to the tin currency of Bombay, Mr. Richard Sainthill writes:—"Ruding in his Supplement, Plate V., and in his second Supplement, Plate 15, gives engravings of some silver and copper coins of Charles II. and James II. of Bombay currency; also a large lead piece of Bombay, which has no date, but from the letters on it (G. R.,) he assigns it with every probability to George I. I have a similar coin, with the date 1741, weight 1 ounce 6 grains; and another with the date 1771, weighing 15 dwts. 15 grains; and I have seen two pieces of similar type and metal, half their size. The coin of 1741 came to me from Dublin; that of 1771 was found a few years since at Kinsale, in repairing a house. These three specimens in lead, being of the reigns of George I., II., and III. from their succession would seem to indicate some established and continuous purpose. It is unlikely that anything honorary would be struck in so worthless and easily injured a metal as lead; yet, as they all bear the authoritative inscription, "Auspice Regis et Senatus Angliæ," we may presume, in the absence of any information, that they were current coins."†

This extract, interesting in many points, as it gives not only weights of the coins, but also a successive series of issues and their divisions during three reigns, commits the error, notwithstanding, of calling lead what is but tutenag and tin mixed in a given proportion, on the Portuguese plan, whose imitation it is in metal, though not in type.

It is, doubtless, a worthless metal, and that was the characteristic quality of the 'material' which made it so acceptacle to the Portuguese in their settlements for petty transactions, the earliest tutenag moneys coined for circulation by the Portùguese in India for this purpose being the pieces called 'roda' and 'bazarucco.'

The *bazaruccada*, as the lot of this worthless coinage was called then, held in all affairs of traffic the same position that *damṛi* did amongst the natives of Southern India. This *damṛi* has a curious deri-

* The *Indian Antiquary*, Bombay. 1882. Vol, XI., p. 13.

† The *Numismatic Chronicle*, Lond. 1855-56. Vol. XVIII., p. 77.

vation, being traced up to a Greek source. *Damṛi* (*Hindustani* دمری) is derived from the Hindu द्रम्म (dramma), worth $\frac{1}{8}$ of a paisa, and the latter is said to be equivalent to the Greek δραχμη, which it does in reality much resemble. But what is the origin of the term *bazarucco?* Mr. H. H. Wilson writes, speaking of *budgrooks*, the English equivalent of the Portuguese *bazarucco*, thus :—" This name has never found a place in any of the accounts of the Indian coins published by the traders to the East Indies, and its meaning and origin are entirely unknown."*

Mr. J. A. Mandelslo, referring to Persia, writes:—"They have a copper coin named *besorg*, 10 of which make 1 *peys*, and again 10 of the latter make one *chay*, the value of which is five *sols* of French money."† To the word *besorg*, then, one may trace the Portuguese *bazarucco*, just as the *xerafim* has already been to *ashrafi*. Besorg is most probably a mutilation or a corruption in the mouth of foreign travellers, of the Persian *bāzār* (بازار) 'the market,' and *rok* (روک) small money, 'change,' the compound word meaning 'small money for bāzār,' just what the word *bazarucco* would be applied to. With regard to the first component part of the term, *rokra paisá*, or ready money, small change, is still used in our Indian markets. Could this be the surviving equivalent of *bāzārok*, or at least of *rok?*

The end of the reign of D. João V. also marks another important historical fact—the complete decadence of the Portuguese power in the East, and under a numismatic point of view, the extinction of most of their mints.

When their star was in the ascendant, and consequently they in the zenith of their energy and vitality, the Portuguese held dominion over the Eastern Coast of Africa, the Persian Gulf, the Malabar Coast, Ceylon, the Malay Peninsula to the confines of China. The *quinas* then floated over the following fortified towns:—Ormus, Diu, Damão, Goa, Bassein, Chaul, Hanowar, Mangalore, Cannanore, Cranganore, Cochin, Coriate, Calaiate, Colombo, Malacca, Ternate, Tidore, Amboina, Macao, Solor and Timor. Out of these towns, eight had established in them mints, which issued money more or less regularly, in gold, silver, copper and tutenag, but two of them in the last two metals only, until

---

* Rev. R. Ruding's *Annals of the Coinage of Great Britain, &c.*, Lond. 1840. Vol. II., p. 418.

† *Ut supra*, p. 32.

the forcible abolition through their capture by the Dutch. The following were the mint marks of six of these towns :—

B .... Bassein.
C—Lo .... Ceylon.
D .... Damão.
D, or D—O... Diu.
G, or G—A ... Goa.
M, or M—A... Malacca.

No mark of the Chaul and Cochin mints has yet been made out, although the *Archivo Portuguez Oriental* contains authentic documents relating to their foundation and their operations, besides preserving for posterity interesting decrees and proclamations referring to various coinages and changes in the value of money. At the time these eight mints were striking money, bearing on one of their sides the cross of the Order of Christ, and circulating throughout their Eastern settlements, the Portuguese sovereigns were proclaiming to the world their title of "Lords of the Commerce, Navigation and Conquests of Ethiopia, Arabia, Persia, and India," which title their successors have not yet ceased to use.*

In course of time the Portuguese Empire in the East began to disintegrate. The first to get loose was Ormus, that famous city, of which, when describing the devil's throne in Pandemonium, Milton writes :—

> "Outshone the wealth of Ormus and of Ind,"

And about which a Russian proverb says :—

> "Whatever is produced on earth you find at Ormus."

Ormus was followed by Malacca, Ceylon, Cochin and other places to the south of Goa, about the middle of the XVIIth century, some places about ten years before, and some as many years after the middle of that century. And lastly, in 1739 and 1740, during the reign of D. João V., were Bassein and Chaul lost. The last coin we have of this "Province of the North," as it was called, is a tutenag piece of 1723, with the

* To lovers of historical parallels or analogies it may be of interest to learn that the ceremonial with which this title was proclaimed more than three centuries ago did not fall short in *eclat* and grandeur of that of the Delhi Assembly of our own time which proclaimed Her Most Gracious Majesty Queen Victoria "Empress of India." And the tenacity with which the Portuguese monarchs hold fast to it is not less remarkable than that with which the English sovereigns from Henry VIII. downwards lay claim to the two letters F. D. (Fidei Defensor) after their names.

mint marks D—B (Damão and Bassein). (See Plate V., fig. 25.) Goa was, indeed, the capital city of all these settlements. King D. Manuel was right when, by his *alvará*, dated the 1st of March 1518, he declared that Goa was "Realenga e nunca seja apartada da Coroa dos nossos reinos," the English equivalent being "royal and never be separated from the crown of our kingdom."* Goa then may be named the metropolitan mint, while the others were provincial ones of this old colonial empire of the Portuguese in the East. I need not mention the African Coasts, although Mozambique, Mombaça, rios de Senna were all supplied with money coined at Goa and Diu, until their separation, in the last century, from the supreme authority at Goa. Now the Portuguese in India were reduced to only two mints, Goa and Diu, that of Damão being temporarily suspended, and then revived again for a short time for issuing copper coinage only, and where the Goa money was uncurrent,—another absurdity of the financial system of the Portuguese in the East! But in their mint towns the Portuguese did not confine themselves to their own coinage; they allowed the approved coinage of the neighbouring princes to circulate in all their settlements, although the names of coins were considerably mangled and altered to the extent of not being easily recognised. An instance of this is to be found in a Gujarati gold piece, which was current at Diu in the early days of the conquest, and was by the Portuguese called *Madrafazão*. Such a term has all the appearance of a foreign origin and import, and it was indeed the corruption of a gold-mohur of Muzafar Shah, one of the kings of Gujarat, whose coin was in his honour called *Muzafarshahi*, just as the gold mohur of Akbar is still called *Akbari*. To this *Muzafarshahi*, then, has the Portuguese *madra fazão* been traced back, not without spending some useful time. Besides, wherever the Portuguese got a footing, there they introduced foreign coins. In Ceylon in 1517 they introduced pagodes, pardaos, xerafins and larins.†

* *O Gabinete Litterario das Fontainhas.* Nova Goa, 1846; Vol. I., p. 22. This letter was confirmed by D. João III., the immediate successor of D. Manuel.

† With regard to the word *pagode*, I have already alluded to all the origins possible of this name, but, as an illustration of how fanciful etymologies are sometimes invented by ingenious writers, I give below a few of them:—

"Amongst the names they have given to the Planets that of Mercury is *Pout*, a Persian word, which signifies an *Idol*, from whence comes *Pout-gheda*, a temple of false gods, and Pagoda comes from *Pout-gheda*."—*New Relation of the Kingdom of Siam*, by Mons. de La Lorbere, Lond. 1693, p. 18. "On n'appelle un temple *Indian Pagode*, que par corruption de *Podghed*, où le mot *Pod* or *Bod* signifie l'object du culte, la divinité. Le nom de *Bud-tan* donné

King D. José I.

D. Francisco de Assis de Tavora,

Viceroy from 1750 to 1754.

The first viceroy of king D. José came to India in 1750, when D. João V. was yet alive. But a royal letter, dated the 5th of August 1750, announcing the death of D. João V., and the proclamation of D. José I., reached Goa on the 24th September 1751. On the 19th of November following solemn funeral obsequies were performed at the Cathedral, and José I. was proclaimed king on the 1st of December. The official mourning continued after the four days spent in rejoicing and festivities of the occasion, and the viceroy closed the proceedings by his reply to the king on the 23rd of January 1752. It would seem now-a-days very strange that what is done at present in a couple of months should only a little more than a century ago occupy the long time from August 1750 to January 1752. These long delays in transmission of despatches from Lisbon to Goa, and *vice versa*, account for the silver coinage of 1751 bearing the busts and legends of both D. João V. and D. José I., although D. João V. had ceased to live in the year 1750. One of the first measures relating to the East of the ministry of D. José I., after his accession to the throne, was the separation of Mozambique and its dependencies in Eastern Africa from the Government of India, by the royal letter dated the 9th of May 1752.

The viceroy caused no alteration to be made in the coinage current in the time of his predecessor, money in gold and silver was continuously issued from the Goa and Diu mints of the same standard as that of the former governors, the only difference being in designs, due to the proclamation of a new king.

Of the gold coins of the period, S. Thomés and their fractions, only one specimen of the former, issued from the mint at Diu, is known to be extant. It bears on one side the cross of St. Thomas with the year

---

au Tibet, veut précisement dire le pays de Dieu, par rapport à la résidence du Dalaï-Lama, en qui l'esprit de Toë est censé résider, et où une grande partie de la Tartarie adore par cette raison."—D' Anville's *Eclaircissemens Géographiques*, &c., Paris, 1753, pp. 75—76. "The word pagoda is a corruption of *Bhaga-vati*, 'holy house,' one of the several names by which Hindu temples are known."—The *Penny Magazine*, June 30th, 1832, p. 122. The derivation of the *pagoda*, given by Bartolomeo, who lived in India from 1776 to 1789, and whose MSS. I saw preserved at the Biblioteca Vittorio Emanuele in Rome, is also from Bhaga-vati, and the one adopted by Dr. Bidie of Madras in his paper on the *pagodas* to the Bengal Asiatic Society.

LAMINA VII

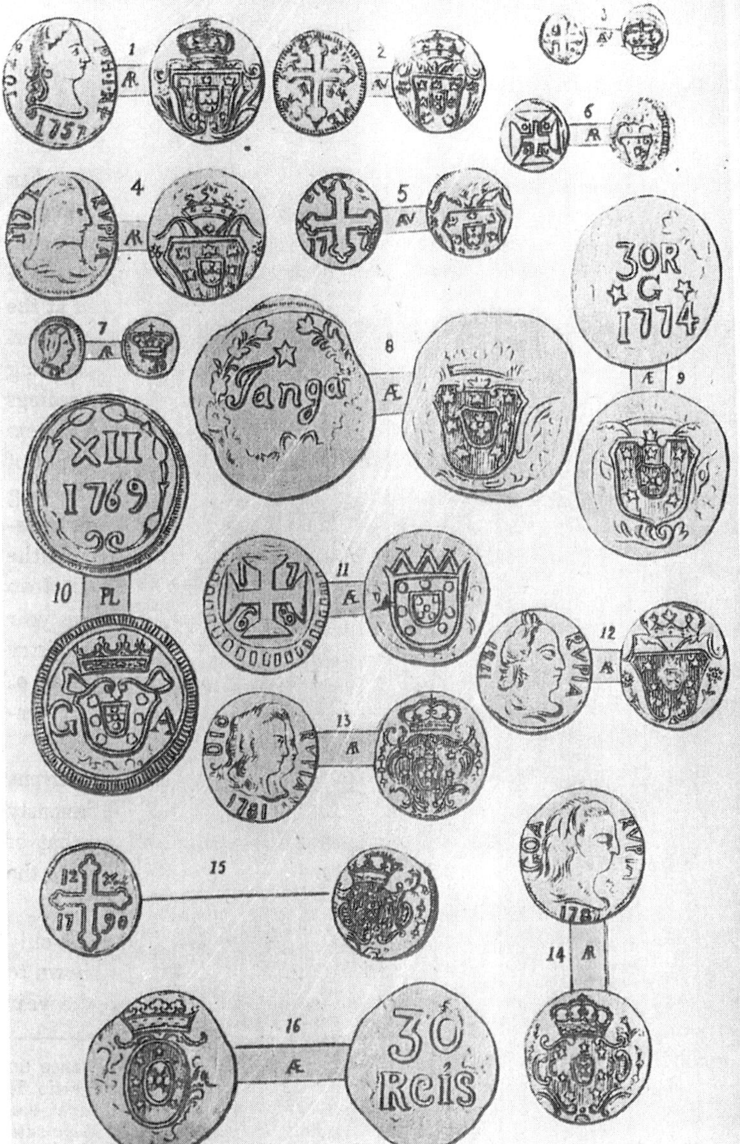

1
Æ
1757
2
AV
3
4
Æ
RVPIA
5
AV
6
Æ
30R
G
1774
Æ 9
7
Æ
8
Æ
Tanga
XIII
1769
10 PL
G A
11
Æ
12
Æ
RVPIA
13
Æ
1781
15
12
17 90
14
Æ
16
Æ
30
Reis

divided into two parts by the lower limb of the cross, and the coat-of-arms of the kingdom on the other.

The silver coinage consisted of rupees and their sub-divisions.

Obv.—Laureate bust of the king with the legend IOZEPH. I. R. P. (Josephus I., Rex Portugaliæ) round the margin. The year 1752 in the exergue.

Rev.—The coat-of-arms of the kingdom. Silver. *Rupia*. Weight, 184 grains Troy. (See Plate VII., fig. 1.)

The sub-divisions of the rupee, *pardao* and *meio pardao* did not differ in type from the rupee; while the *tanga* and *meia tanga* bore designs similar to those of the corresponding coins of the reign of D. João V. Indeed, some of these pieces give no indication at all, except when they bear in the exergue the date,—and to which pieces I shall have to refer hereafter,—of the reign or governorship during which they were struck, as was once the case with the silver *vintem* at Lisbon, which bore one invariable design from the time of D. João V. to that of D. João VI., more than a century.

In the archives of the mint at Lisbon, a list is preserved of the coins in gold, silver, copper, and tutenag current in Portuguese India and at Mozambique, issued from the mints of Goa and Diu, with their nomenclature, designs, standard, &c., which is very interesting for the numismatic history of the time. It is dated 1753.

D. Luiz Mascarenhas.

1754—1756.

During this short period coins in gold and silver were issued both from the Goa and the Diu mints. They did not differ in any way from those of his predecessor. On the death of this viceroy, a triple provisional commission, presided over by the archbishop of the time, governed the country from 1756 to 1758, but made no change in the contemporary money.

Manuel de Saldanha de Albuquerque,

1758—1765.

This viceroy commanded during his time the issue of money in gold, silver, copper and tutenag. Of the gold coinage the S. Thomés of the value of 12 xerafins, with the sub-divisions of eight, four, and two xerafins were struck.

Obv.—The coat-of-arms of the kingdom.

Rev.—The cross of St. Thomas in the field, with the legend CR DE-ST-ME. round the margin. (CRus De S. ThoME.) The lower limb of the cross divides the year 1764 into two parts. *Grénetis.* Gold. *S. Thomé.* Weight, 75 grains Troy. (See Plate VII., fig. 2.) This specimen is in my collection. The fractional specimens of the S. Thomé are not obtainable. I remember having seen one of the value of four xerafins in the collection of the Hon'ble Mr. J. Gibbs, with a design resembling somewhat one kind of the silver tangas published during this period.

Of the silver coinage issued from 1756 to 1765, there were *rupia, pardao, meio pardao, tanga, and meia tanga.* The designs of the first three did not differ in any essential point from those of the former governors, except that the legend in 1761 was changed into Portuguese IOZE-PRIM (EIRO) instead of the Latin one of 1751. Two specimens of the *meio pardao* of this type are extant, as far as hitherto known.

The *tangas* bore three different designs, and the *meias tangas* two. In fact these designs appear to have been common to several more or less interrupted periods, with very slight variations. Of the present ruler we have the examples of a *tanga* with the bust of the king and the date in the exergue on one side, and the numeral 60, value in reis, under a crown on the other ; and of the *meia tanga*, exactly the same type, except the numeral 30 on the reverse, representative of its value in reis. The copper and tutenag coinages were varied and numerous in design, size and standard, to which may be added the novelty of the issue of bronze pieces with the addition of tin in a certain proportion ; but this subject does not offer any great interest to the numismatist, as it perhaps did to the merchant of the period, for the innovation suffered such an opposition from the public that the viceroy was at last obliged to give up the bronze pieces and return to the old tutenag ones. It is, however, worth mentioning that of the copper coinage there were ten kinds of pieces, viz. :—2 tangas, tanga, meia tanga, vintem, 15 reis, 12, 10, 6, 5, and 2½ ; while of the tutenag one there were only three, 15 reis, 10, and 5.

1765—1768.

On the departure of the viceroy Manuel de Saldanha to Lisbon, a triple provisional commission was nominated to govern the country, their rule being extended beyond one's expectation, owing to the coming viceroy, Conde da Louzã, having died on his voyage to India.

During this government gold, silver, copper and tutenag were coined into S. Thomés, rupias, meia tangas and bazaruccos, with their subdivisions. Of the first there were pieces of 12 xerafins, 8, 4, and 2. Of this series the following specimen is a good example :—

Obv.—The coat-of-arms of the kingdom.

Rev.—The cross of St. Thomas in the field, having in its upper angles 2—x (indicative of its value in xerafins), and the year 1766 in the lower ones. Gold. Weight, 12 grains Troy. In my collection. (See Plate VII., fig. 3.) Of the copper and tutenag coinage, as well as of the silver ones, I reserve to speak at the end of the reign of D. José I., as they do not appear to differ much from the types already described.

D. Joao Jose' de Mello,

1768—1774.

Although money in gold, silver, copper, and tutenag was struck in the Goa mint as well as in that of Diu, it did not present any new type, nor was the standard altered. The tutenag bazaruccos were issued in greater quantity than before, as they were a source of profit to the Government. To the copper pieces bearing the date 1774 I shall refer further on.

On the death of the governor, D. João José de Mello, which took place on the 10th of January 1774, Filippe de Valladares Soutomaior was appointed Governor of Portuguese India, who laid down the reins of the Government on the 24th of September 1774. Of his very short rule we have but a copper coinage of meia tanga, vintem, and meio vintem, of which more hereafter. If gold and silver as well as tutenag were continued to be coined into current money or not there are no available documents to confirm one's supposition either way.

D. Jose' Pedro da Camara,

1774—1779.

This is an important period under a numismatic point of view. We have a series of coins in gold, silver, and tutenag, the latter two struck both at Goa and at Diu. The copper coinage was not issued anew, as that of the former governor's time was enough.

Of the gold pieces there were S. Thomés of 12 xerafins, of 8, 4 and 2 of a new type.

Obv.—The coat-of-arms of the kingdom.

Rev.—Cross of St. Thomas, the lower limb shorter than usual. Round the margin the legend OTTO XERAFINS, with a star between the two words. The year 1778 on the sides of the lower limb of the cross. Gold. *S. Thomé.* Weight, 74 grains Troy. (See Plate VII., fig. 5.)

Of the silver coinage there were the rupia and its fractions, except perhaps the *meia tanga*, of which minute coinage there was a sufficient quantity issued by former governors. The type of the rupee was altered, the sub-divisions of the rupee following suit.

Obv.—The bust of the king to the right, having before him the word RUPIA, and behind the year 1777. Silver. *Rupia.* Weight, 162 grains Troy. (See Plate VII., fig. 4.)

The year 1777 was the last of the memorable reign of D. José I., more remarkable for the very useful, although violent, measures of his great minister, the Marquis de Pombal, than for any high and estimable quality in the king himself.

Of the tangas and meias tangas of this reign here are two specimens.

Obv.—The coat-of-arms of the kingdom.

Rev.—A cross of the Order of Christ, having a star in each angle. Silver. *Tanga.* Weight, 15 grains Troy. (See Plate VII., fig. 6.)

The other types of the tanga of this reign were, first, the laureate bust of the king between two palms, with the year in the exergue on one side, and the royal crown with the value of the piece on the other; second, the same obverse, the reverse being an ornamented coat-of-arms of the kingdom; third, the value of the coin below the royal crown on one side, and the cross of the Order of Christ with the stars in its angles on the other.

Of the *meia tanga*, the following piece is a fine specimen :—

Obv.—Bust of the king to the right, and the year (17)64 in the exergue.

Rev.—30, the value in reis of the coin, above it the royal crown. Silver. *Meia tanga.* Weight, 10 grains Troy. (See Plate VII., fig. 7.)

The other variety of this kind of silver piece is the bust of the king to the right, without the date of issue, the reverse being the same as above.

The copper coinage of this reign is also varied in type, numerous in the serial order of fractional pieces, some pieces being voluminous in size, with a corresponding heaviness in weight.

The largest copper piece of this reign is the *tanga*, which had its sub-divisions of *meia tanga*, 20 reis and 10 reis.

Obv.—The coat-of-arms of the kingdom.

Rev.—*Tanga* in the field, surrounded by a laurel wreath, having on the top a star. Copper. *Tanga.* Weight, 10 drachms 30 grains Troy. (See Plate VII., fig. 8.)

The other type of the copper coinage is the one dated 1774. It consists of 30, 20, 12, 10 and 6 reis.

Obv.—The coat-of-arms of the kingdom.

Rev.—G (Goa) between two stars in the field, having 30 R. (representative of the value in reis) above, and the year 1774 below, all encircled by a laurel crown. Copper. *Meia tanga.* Weight, 5 drachms Troy. (See Plate VII., fig. 9.)

Of the tutenag coinage of the reign, of which there was also a graduated series of 15, 12, 10, 6, 5, 4, and 2 reis, perhaps even 1 real. The following example will be sufficient :—

Obv.—The coat-of-arms of the kingdom between the letters G—A (Goa).

Rev.—The numeral XII., indicative of its value in reis, with the year 1769 below it, all within a wreath. Tutenag. 12 *Reis.* Weight, 3 drachms 30 grains Troy. (See Plate VII., fig. 10.)

Some years the numeral was represented in Roman figures, and other in Arabic ones.

From the Diu mint were issued copper pieces of graduated value in reis, of which the following specimen is a typical example :—

Obv.—The coat-of-arms of the kingdom between the letter D—O (Dio).

Rev.—Cross of the Order of Christ,' having in the angles the figures 1768 of the year of its issue. Copper., 5 *Reis.* Weight, 2 drachms 15 grains Troy. (See Plate VII., fig. 11.)

From the same mint were also issued tutenag pieces, the largest of which is already illustrated at Plate I., fig. 7. All the specimens above described and illustrated are in my collection.

About the middle of 1777 arrived at Goa the sad news of the death of D. José I., and the accession to the Portuguese throne of D. Maria I., his daughter.

D. Maria I.,

1777—1799.

D. José Pedro da Camara continued to govern the country until the 26th of May 1779, during which time he commanded the issue of some copper pieces, to be considered in the government of his successor, who was

D. Frederico Guilrerme de Sousa,

1779—1786.

During this time, money was coined in gold, silver and copper. The gold S. Thomés and their sub-divisions bore the same designs as those to be described hereafter, for, from this date until the cessation of the gold coinage, they were not altered at all. The fractions of the S. Thomés of 12 xerafins were those of 8, 4 and 2 xerafins.

With regard to the silver coinage, the *rupia* and its sub-divisions of pardao, and meio pardao were issued. Of the issue of the tanga and meia tanga there is still some uncertainty.

Obv.—The laureate bust of the queen to the right in the centre, with 1781 on one side and RUPIA on the other.

Rev.—The coat-of-arms of the kingdom. Silver. *Rupia.* Weight, 165 grains Troy. (See Plate VII., fig. 12.)

In the same year the Diu mint issued rupees with two busts.

Obv.—The laureate busts of the queen and her husband to the right in the middle, having DIO behind and RUPIA in front. 1781 in the exergue.

Rev.—The coat-of-arms of the kingdom. Silver. *Rupia de Diu.* Weight, 161 grains Troy. (See Plate VII., fig. 13.)

The whole of the early silver coinage of Queen D. Maria I., issued from the Goa mint, bore the rupee type, changing only the designation of the coin as pardao and meio pardao, and, perhaps, as 60 and 30 reis for the tanga and meia tanga. It was from 1782 that the two busts began to make their appearance on the silver coinage struck in the Goa mint, bearing on the obverse the words Goa and Rupia in front and behind the profiles; while the date of the issue was placed in the exergue.

The double busts, first struck at Diu, represent the Queen, D. Maria I. and her husband, who was also her uncle, D. Pedro III. These double bust coins bear no inconsiderable resemblance in this respect to those of William and Mary of England, issued just a century before. Although the same style of coinage in its general appearance, fineness and weight as when the queen was unmarried, the difference now consisted only in the profiles of the king and queen being shown one over the other, without any legend relating to the two personages, as was also the case with the coins of William and Mary.

These double bust coins were continued issuing even more than a year after the death of D. Pedro III., which took place on the 25th of May 1786. After the death of her husband, the queen's bust appears alone, from 1788, and was so continued for about one year after her decease.

The copper coinage of this period consisted of tanga, meia tanga, vintem, 12, 6, 4½, 3, and 1½ reis. These coins bore on one side the ornamented coat-of-arms of the kingdom, and their value, as $\frac{60}{\textit{Reis}}$ one above the other in the field of the reverse, encircled by a laurel wreath.

During this Government Goa was afflicted with heaps of false money in copper and tutenag introduced from abroad, which compelled the governor, as well as his predecessor from 1774, to reform the standard of coins, to order the recoining of this coinage, and alter frequently the designs, which accounts for the varied types still extant, attributable often to the same year.

Francisco da Cunha e Menezes.

1786—1794.

Of this governor we have S. Thomés and some sub-divisions as above, rupees with the same fractions, and copper pieces of tanga, meia tanga, and vintem.

The style of S. Thomés was not altered in any way, but the silver coinage, represented by the rupee, was as follows:—

O

Obv.—Bust of the queen in the middle to the right, with a widows' veil. GOA behind, and RVPIA in front of the bust. The year 1787 in the exergue.

Rev.—The ornamented coat-of-arms of the kingdom. Silver. *Rupia.* Weight, 165 grains Troy. (See Plate VII., fig. 14.)

The gold coinage, represented by the S. Thomé, had only one type for nearly half a century, or until its abolition in the Goa mint, and it may be illustrated by the following specimen:—

Obv.—The coat-of-arms of the kingdom with the shield, ornamented all round.

Rev.—Cross of S. Thomé, having in its upper angles 12-x, indicative of its value, as 12 xerafins, and below the four numerals 1790. Gold. *S. Thomé.* Weight, 75 grains Troy. (See Plate VII., fig. 15.)

Of the copper coinage, there is nothing remarkable to notice, except that the reverse bears the full designation of the coin, for instance, *Tangá*, and below it the date 1787, while the obverse has the usual coat-of-arms of the kingdom. There may have been issued other fractions of the tanga, besides the two above mentioned; as also tutenag pieces might have been struck during the time of this governor, but no specimens are found which may be appropriated to this period.

Francisco Antonio da Veiga Cabral,

1794—1807.

During this period the Goa mint was active in coining money in gold, silver and copper of the kind already described, with the addition of S. Thomés of the value of 1 xerafim; while the Diu mint struck silver rupees, its halves and quarters, copper *atiás* and tutenag bazaruccos, in a series of 20, 10, 5, and 3 bazaruccos. These latter have been sufficiently illustrated, the silver coinage alone requires a short notice here.

Obv.—The ornamented coat-of-arms of the kingdom.

Rev.—Cross of St. Thomas in the middle, the four numerals 1806 in the angles, having 600, indicative of the value in reis, in the top, and Dio at the bottom, ornamentation round the margin. Silver. *Rupia.* Weight, 115 grains Troy. (See Plate VIII., fig. 1.)

Of the copper coinage issued from the Goa mint, the following specimen of *meia tanga* is typical.

Obv.—The ornamented coat-of-arms of the kingdom.

Rev.—In the field in two lines 30-Reis. Copper. *Meia tanga.* Weight, 4 drachms 25 grains Troy (See Plate VII., fig. 16.)

During this Government, Queen D. Maria I. was declared *non compos mentis*, and her son D. João *principe regente* by the decree dated the 15th of July 1799. The latter ruled the kingdom as a reigning prince until the demise of his queen-mother, which took place on the 20th of March 1816, was proclaimed king on the 16th of February 1818, and died in 1826. He had before this held the reins of the kingdom in the name of the queen from the 10th of February 1792 to the 15th of July 1799. This was the most unfortunate time for Portugal and her colonies.

When everything was neglected, it is not to be expected that the mints of Goa and Diu, the only remnants of a once large array of colonial monetary establishments, should merit any special attention to the rulers or authorities of the time. The queen, always surrounded by an *entourage* of dangerously irresponsible mystics, who had fattened on the carcass of the old Portugal, and who, according to a national historian, were like the Termites eating to the bone that once noble people, had been by them declared a *beata*, literally 'blessed,' but truly a fanatic. She eventually became mad; for from fanaticism to madness there is but one step. Her son, the only son of a mad woman, was imbecile, as was very natural; in 1808 he sought safety from the Napoleonic invasion of the peninsula in the flight to Brazil.* If from Lisbon the government of the colonies was far from satisfactory, one can easily imagine what the state of these new settlements must have been now that the court and ministry were at Rio de Janeiro. But to return to the chronicle of the issues of money.

D. Joao VI.,

As regent from 1799 to 1818.
As king from 1818 to 1826.

The first governor of the regency was the one above mentioned, but he was succeeded in 1807 by

Bernardo José Maria de Lorena.

1807—1816.

This viceroy issued the same kind of coins as his predecessor, only his silver coinage showed a new design, well represented by the Rupia.

* Cf. *Historia de Portugal*; by J. P. Oliveira Martins. Lisbon: 1879. Vol. II., pp. 158, *et seq.*

Obv.—The laureate bust of the prince regent to the right, RVPIA D GOA around, and 1807 in the exergue.

Rev.—Ornamented coat-of-arms of the kingdom with the oval shield. Silver. *Rupia.* Weight, 2 drachms 45 grains Troy. (See Plate VIII., fig. 2.)

This type of the silver coinage is said to date from the time of the governor Veiga Cabral, omitting the letter D.

Of the gold coinage, the following is a good example :—

Obv.—The reverse of the coin last described.

Rev.—Cross of St. Thomas, having in the lower angles 18-12, and in the upper 12-x, the value of the coin. Gold. *S. Thomé.* Weight, 75 grains Troy. (See Plate VIII., fig 3.)

A peculiarity of the numismatic history of this time is the irregularity not only in the often unsystematic arrangement of the coins regarding their designs and standard, but also the simultaneous issue of coins bearing busts or profiles of both the mother and son separately.

Although coins bearing the bust of the mad queen were struck and issued until about a year after her death, those of the prince regent were also current. A rupee and a meia tanga are extant which bear on the obverse not only the laureate bust of the prince but also the legend D. IOAO P. G. D. P. R. on the silver piece, while on the copper one it runs JOANNES. D. G. PORT. ET. ALG. P. REGENS and the year 1814 in the exergue. But these were most probably not current coins but mere patterns ; for it is very strange that from so recent a time there should exist only two specimens in two metals.

D. Diogo de Souza,

1817—1821.

During this time money in gold, silver, and copper was coined of all the varieties already mentioned, except the silver *meia tanga*, which had ceased to be struck for some time previous to the present government. The gold S. Thomés and their fractions bore the same type above described ; but the silver coinage presented a new design, which is represented by the rupee, as follows :—

Obv.—Bust of the prince regent to the right, the legend GOA—RVPIA behind and in the front of the bust, respectively, and the year 1817 in the exergue.

LÂMINA VIII

Rev.—The arms of the United Kingdom, *i. e.* the coat-of-arms of Portugal with the sphere of Brazil. Silver. *Rupia.* Weight, 170 grains Troy. (See Plate VIII., fig 4.)

This was the type of the last coinage of the regency, to be followed by that of the reign of D. João VI., who from the condition of prince regent was solemnly proclaimed king on the 16th of February 1818. Now his profile appears considerably altered for the worse, but whether it is the defect of workmanship, or that the physiognomy of D. João VI. had in the interim become idiotic since his flight to Brazil, one cannot say. Here is, however, his coin of the time :—

Obv.—Bust of the king to the right with the legend as in the coin last described, and the year 1818 in the exergue.

Rev.—The coat-of-arms of the United Kingdom. Silver. *Rupia.* Weight, 165 grains Troy. (See Plate VIII., fig. 5.)

Of the copper coinage of the period, the following specimen of the *tangas*, representative of two series of copper coins issued about this time, will give a correct idea.

Obv.—Ornamented coat-of-arms of the United Kingdom.

Rev.—In the field, in two lines, 60-Reis. Copper. *Tanga.* Weight, 9 drachms 45 grains Troy. (See Plate VIII., fig. 6.)

Obv.—The ornamented coat-of-arms of the kingdom with the oval shield.

Rev.—In the field, in three lines, 60-Reis-1818. Copper. *Tanga.* Weight, 8 drachms 37½ grains Troy. (See Plate VIII., fig. 7.)

The Diu mint does not show us during this period any product of its activity except the tutenag bazaruccos of the type and standard already described. It is said that the copper coinage bearing in the field the year 1818 was struck at Diu ; but this is doubtful.

On account of a revolt at Goa, both before and after the departure of the viceroy D. Diogo de Souza to Rio de Janeiro on the 4th of March 1822, a first provisional commission, composed of four persons, governed Portuguese India from September to December 1821, and a second, consisting of six individuals, from the latter date to November 1823, when the president of the second commission was nominated viceroy. During this revolutionary period, on account of changes in the Home Government from absolutism to constitutional regimen, the mints both at Goa and Diu were nearly closed.

D. Manuel da Camara,

1823—1825.

During the three years gold, silver and copper coins were issued from the mint at Goa, but the standard type and module were the same as of the preceding years.

This viceroy died at Goa on the 16th of November 1825, when a provisional commission, composed of three gentlemen, held the reins of the Government until the arrival of the newly-appointed viceroy, which took place on the 9th of October 1826. During this short interval no change took place in the monetary matters of Portuguese India.

In the last year of the rule of this commission, King D. João VI. died, being succeeded by

D. Pedro IV.,

1826—1828.

Viceroy D. Manuel de Portugal e Castro.

1826—1835.

This was a period fruitful of political changes, and of considerable activity in the improvement of the colonial coinage, which had now exceeded all measure of rudeness in workmanship. Among political changes was the proclamation of the Constitutional Charter in the city of Goa on the 18th of October 1827, and of D. Pedro IV., king of Portugal, who had succeeded his father, D. João VI., on the 10th of March 1826. This distinguished prince abdicated the crown on behalf of his daughter, D. Maria, on the 2nd of May 1826, which abdication was ratified on the 2nd of March 1828. He then declared himself regent of the kingdom on the 3rd of March 1832 until the 19th of September 1834, or until the pretender to the throne, D. Miguel de Bragança, was completely defeated.

Money was coined in Goa and Diu, gold, silver, bronze and copper in the former place, and tutenag in the latter. The gold specimens of the period are extremely rare. Of silver the following example is typical:—

Obv.—Laureate bust of the monarch to the right, having the year 1831 in the exergue.

Rev.—Coat-of-arms of the United Kingdom. Silver. ***Rupia.*** Weight, 170 grains Troy. (See Plate VIII., fig. 8.)

Of the bronze coinage there were only tangas and half tangas.

Obv.—The coat-of-arms of the kingdom in the field.

Rev.—Within a crown AP. (Asia Portuguese) and T under it (Tanga). Bronze. *Tanga.* Weight, 9 drachms 55½ grains Troy. (See Plate VIII., fig. 9.)

The *meia tanga* bears the same design, there being the addition of ½ between the letters AP. and T. to indicate its value. The type of the copper coinage did not differ at all from that of the bronze one, except that portion of it which was ordered to be countermarked, on account of the false copper money introduced from abroad into the country.

Obv—The same as of the coin last described.

Rev.—Also the same, the countermarks being PR. and 809 below it. Copper. *Tanga.* Weight, 9 drachms 35 grains Troy. (See Plate VIII., fig. 12.)

There being scantiness of copper pieces in Diu, some of the half tangas struck and current at Goa at this time were marked with the word Dio to the left of the letters abovementioned for circulation at that place. Two specimens of this currency, as well as the specimens above described and illustrated, are in my collection.

With regard to the countermark PR. and 809, it appears that PR. stands for Principe Regente, while 809 is perhaps the year 1809, when the countermarks were first used in Goa.

The viceroy D. Manuel de Portugal, observing the extreme irregularity in the execution of the mintage in Goa, which is evident to any one who may have cursorily examined the colonial coinage of the Portuguese in India, appointed a committee of learned persons, by his decree dated the 30th of July 1828, to report on those irregularities, and to indicate means to improve the condition of the mintage. A report was naturally presented in course of time to the Government, who in 1834 approved the new mint regulations, and commanded the issue of money with designs recommended by the committee. The coins with new designs, however, turned out to be mere patterns, for they were never current. But of this aborted effect of the labours of the committee, and of the causes that led to it, I shall speak more at length hereafter.

D. Maria II., 1834—1853.

The first viceroy of Queen D. Maria II. was the last of her great father; but his coinage of this period was confined to the issue of silver rupees and copper tangas with their respective sub-divisions, which had, however, the misfortune of never forming part of the currency. They were no sooner struck than both the silver and copper pieces were, from political reasons, ordered to be kept in the mint, as mere patterns, of which, as above said, I shall speak further on.

This viceroy was in 1835 followed by Bernardo Peres da Silva, whose extremely short and revolutionary rule made no change in the coinage, and was followed by the first viceroy of the queen again, and then by Marshal Correa, and finally by a Provisional Government from 1835 to 1837. The only monetary document relating to the time of this Government is the order to withdraw from circulation the silver and copper money minted in 1834, and the issue of others instead, bearing the bust of the queen; while the copper coinage, which was now depreciated, was commanded to be struck with the designs of 1832. It was prohibited to receive into the Government Treasury more than one-third of the copper money in payment of the State revenues. This Government was followed by Barão de Sabroso, from 1837 to 1838, who did nothing more than appoint a committee to investigate the causes of the scantiness of the silver money, the depreciation of the copper one, as false coinage in the latter metal was introduced into the country, and to propose measures to facilitate the circulation of gold and silver money. He also ordered the sale of silver plate belonging to the now extinguished convents, except the sacred vessels, and of the product to issue silver coin in rupees and their fractions, and later on the reducing of the plate itself to currency. This governor was succeeded by another Provisional Commission, who ruled from 1838 to 1839, during which short time were issued the following coins in silver and copper:—

Obv.—Bust of the queen to the left, with the legend RUPIA DE GOA around, and the year 1839 in the exergue between two stars.

Rev.—The coat-of-arms of the kingdom between two laurel branches linked below. Silver. *Rupia.* Weight, 165 grains Troy. (See Plate VIII., fig. 10.)

Of the sub-divisions of the rupee there were pardao and meio pardao.

Obv.—The coat-of-arms of the kingdom,

Rev.—60-T. in two lines within two palms wreath, or A P above and T below. Copper. *Tanga.* Weight, 9 drachms 45 grains Troy. (See Plate VIII., fig. 11.)

The *Tanga* had issued along with it the fractions of half, quarter, 12, 7½, 6, and 3 reis.

LAMINA IX

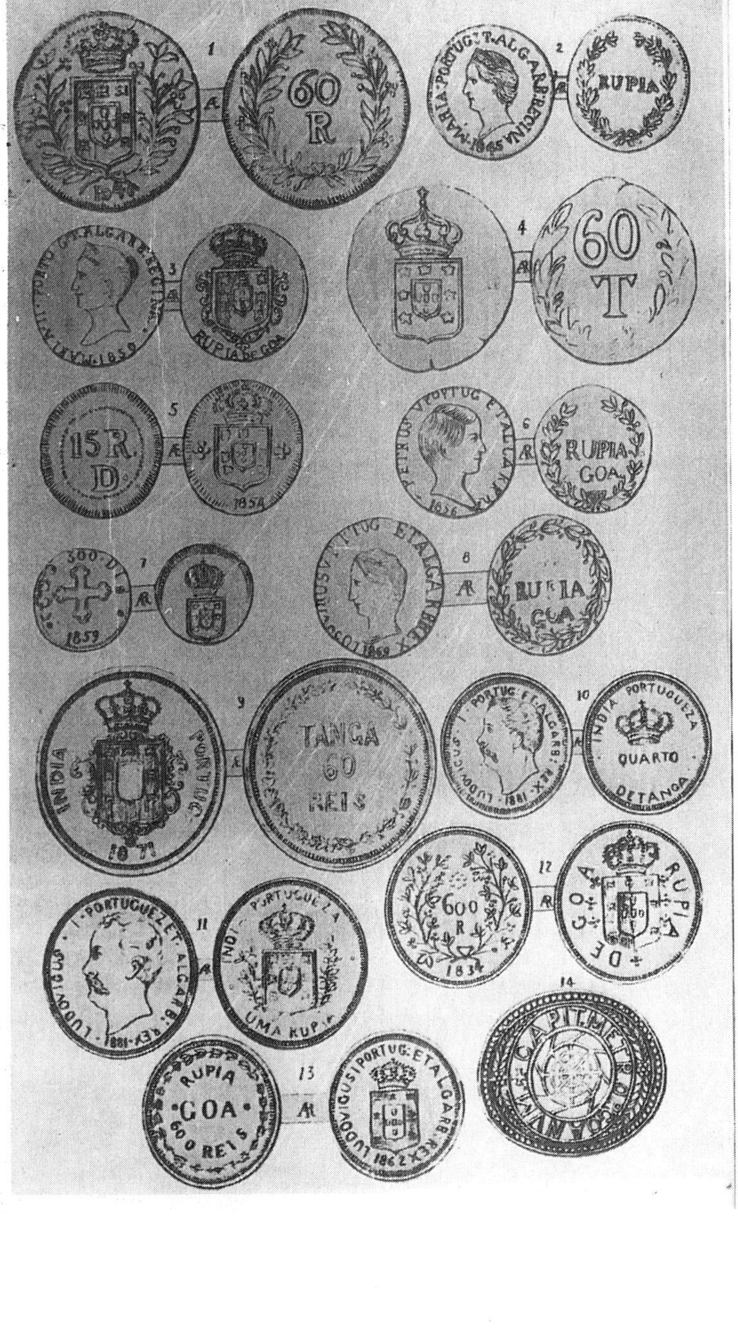

60 R
RUPIA
RUPIA DE GOA
60 T
15 R. D
1854
RUPIA GOA
1859
TANGA 60 REIS
INDIA PORTUGUEZA QUARTO DE TANGA
600 R
RUPIA
UMA RUPIA
RUPIA GOA 600 REIS
LUDOVICUS I PORTUG: ET ALGARB: REX 1862

This last Government was followed also provisionally by Colonel Vieira, until November 1839, who did not alter the coinage, and was succeeded by the governor Manuel José Mendes, who ruled until 1840, and who also did not interfere with the coinage established by former Governments. Then came another Provisional Government until 1840, who ordered both gold and silver ornaments belonging to convents of Goa and Damão, *inclusive* the sacred vessels which had been profaned, to be coined into gold and silver money.

José Joaquim Lopes de Lima,

1840—1842.

During this Government gold, silver, and copper were coined, the first into *S. Thomés*, the second into *rupias*, halves and quarters, and the third into *tangas* and halves.

The S. Thomé, bearing the date 1841, was the last gold coin ever struck at Goa, the type being nearly similar to the one last described of the value of 12 xerafins.

The silver rupee of Diu bore the same design and date as above mentioned; while the Goa copper tanga was as follows:—

Obv.—The coat-of-arms of the kingdom between two laurel branches and the year 1840 in the exergue.

Rev.—60-R. in two lines inside a laurel crown. Copper. *Tanga* Weight, 10 drachms 5 grains Troy. (See Plate IX., fig. 1.)

This governor was followed by another Provisional Government from April to September 1842, when the Governor Conde das Antas took possession of the place, which he occupied till April 1843. The only thing he did with reference to the coinage was to order the closing of the mint, sending the materials to the arsenal, to be there kept until the time when they would again be required for coining purposes. He was succeeded by the governor Joaquim Mourão Garcez Palha, from April 1843 to May 1844, during which time the Damão mint, which had remained closed for nearly a century, was opened again to mint copper money, consisting of tangas, meias tangas and 15 reis. The description of this last coin is thus:—

Obv.—The coat-of-arms of the kingdom between two flowery embellishments, and the year in the exergue.

Rev.—15-R—D. in two lines within a beaded circle. Copper. 15 *Reis.* Weight, 160 grains Troy. (See Plate IX., fig. 5.)

JOSÉ FERREIRA PESTANA,

1844—1851.

The mint of Goa, which had been closed from the 19th of November 1842, was re-opened in 1845 for the minting of silver and copper money, whose types were as follows :—

Obv.—The bust of the queen to the left; the legend MARIA II. PORTUG : ET : ALGARB : REGINA around; in the exergue the year 1845.

Rev.—Inside a laurel crown RUPIA. Silver. *Rupia.* Weight, 168 grains Troy. (See Plate IX., fig. 2.)

Of the silver coinage, besides the rupee, there were issued its half and quarter. The copper pieces consisted of 10, 7½, 6, 4½ and 3 reis. Some of the old tangas, meias tangas, and 15 reis were also recoined with the dies of 1839, on account of the designs having been worn out.

JOSÉ JOAQUIM JANUARIO LAPA,

1851—1855.

During this period, in the middle of which Queen D. Maria II. died, being succeeded by her son D. Pedro V., the only coins struck in the Goa mint were *rupia* and *pardao*, whose designs were thus :—

Obv.—Diademed bust of the queen to the left, MARIA II. PORTUG: ET : ALGARB : REGINA round the margin ; and the year 1851 in the exergue.

Rev.—Ornamented coat-of-arms of the kingdom, the legend RUPIA DE GOA below. Silver. *Rupia.* Weight, 170 grains Troy. (See Plate IX., fig. 3.)

D. PEDRO V.,

1853—1861.

The Governor left India in 1855, being succeeded in the government of the country by a Council composed of four persons, who made no alteration in any of the coinages, and handed over the reins of the Government on the 3rd of November 1855 to

ANTONIO CESAR DE VARCONCELLOS CORREA.

1855—1864.

During this Government silver coins were issued from both the Goa and Diu mints. From the former, rupee, half, quarter, and tanga or

60 reis; from the latter half a rupee and the quarter. Their types were as follows :—

Obv.—The bust of the young king to the right; the year 1856 in the exergue.

Rev.—RUPIA—GOA in two lines in the field inside a laurel crown. Silver. *Rupia.* Weight, 168 grains Troy. (See Plate IX., fig. 6.)

Obv.—The coat-of-arms of the kingdom.

Rev.—St. Thomas's cross, an ornament to the left, Dio to the right. 300, indicative of its value in reis, in the top, and the year 1859 between two stars below. Silver. *Pardao de Diu.* Weight, 60 grains Troy. (See Plate IX., fig. 7.)

This coinage appears to have been the last ever issued from the mint at Diu. In the meantime D. Pedro V. died, being succeeded by his brother, the present monarch, His Most Faithful Majesty

D. Luiz I.

1861.

On the accession to the throne of the present sovereign of Portugal, the last governor of D. Pedro V. continuing to be the governor of Portuguese India, it was proposed to issue a new type of the rupee, which was struck, but never became current. Of this pattern piece I shall again have to speak further on.

José Ferreira Pestana,

1864—1870.

During the second governorship of the above gentleman, the only coinage issued from the Goa mint, and the last ever struck there, was a rupee and its half, the last date being 1869, when the mint was closed. The type of this coinage was as follows :—

Obv.—Bust of the king to the left, and the year 1869 in the exergue.

Rev.—Within a laurel crown the legend RUPIA—GOA in two lines. Silver. *Rupia.* Weight, 165 grains Troy. (See Plate IX., fig. 8.)

Januario Correa de Almeida.

1870—1871.

This gentleman ordered the issue of copper money for Portuguese India from the Bombay mint. The *tanga*, with its fractions of $\frac{1}{2}$, $\frac{1}{4}$, and 10, 5, 3 reis were sent in circulation, the type being as follows :—

Obv.—The coat-of-arms of the kingdom in the field dividing the marginal legend INDIA PORTUG : and the year 1871 in the exergue.

Rev.—Inside a laurel crown the legend in three lines, TANGA—60—REIS in the field. Copper. *Tanga.* Weight, 9 drachms 35 grains Troy. (See Plate IX., fig. 9.)

This governor was in 1871 succeeded by Joaquim José de Macedo e Couto, who ruled till 1875. Then came João Tavares de Almeida, who died in July 1877, being followed by a Government Council until the arrival of the Governor Antonio Sergio de Souza, who ruled from November 1877 and died in May 1878, being succeeded in his turn by another Council, pending the arrival of the next Governor, who was

CAETANO ALEXANDRE DE ALMEIDA E ALBUQUERQUE, 1878—1882.

This, the most remarkable of governments in a numismatic point of view, caused all the Portuguese coinage, even the most recent one, to become absolutely obsolete, by withdrawing it from circulation, and substituting for it the silver and copper coinage first struck at Calcutta and then at Bombay, in consequence of the Monetary Convention of the new Anglo-Portuguese Treaty. General Pearse, a distinguished authority on Indian numismatics, having suggested the publication of the text of the Convention in the body of this paper, and being convinced of the importance of this document for the history of Indo-Portuguese coinages, I have much pleasure in quoting it here as follows :—

CONVENTION.

Whereas, by the fifth article of a Treaty of Commerce and Extradition executed at Lisbon on the twenty-sixth day of December 1878, and ratified on the sixth day of August 1879, between His Most Faithful Majesty the King of Portugal and the Algarves and Her Majesty the Queen of the United Kingdom of Great Britain and Ireland, Empress of India, it is provided that the High Contracting Parties shall use their best endeavours to establish between their respective systems of moneys, weights, and measures the harmony desirable for the development of commercial relations between their respective dominions; and whereas by the same article it is further provided that the detailed measures to be adopted shall form the subject of a separate Convention between the Governors General of British India and Portuguese India, to be executed within two years from the date when the said Treaty comes into force; and whereas the said Treaty came into force on the fifteenth day of January 1880 :

In pursuance of the said article, the following Convention has been made :—

1. The Governor General of Portuguese India shall adopt, in the Portuguese possessions in India, the monetary system of British India, for the time being in force, provided that the coins shall have on one side the effigy of the King

of Portugal, with the legend *Ludovicus I, Portugaliæ et Algarbiorum Rex*, around it, or such other effigy and legend as the said Governor General may from time to time desire, and on the other side the value of each coin, the year of the Christian era, and the words *India Portugueza.*

2. Subject to the provisions of clause 7, so long as this Convention remains in force, the following coins and no others shall be struck for Portuguese India:—

Silver.—Rupee, weighing 180 grains troy;

Half-rupee, weighing 90 grains troy;

Quarter-rupee weighing 45 grains troy;

Eighth of a rupee, weighing 22½ grains troy;

The standard fineness of the said silver coins shall be eleven-twelfths of the fine silver and one-twelfth of alloy, subject to a remedy not exceeding the following:—

	Remedy in weight.	Remedy in fineness.
Rupee	Five thousandths ...	Two thousandths.
Half-rupee		
Quarter-rupee	Seven thousandths ...	Three thousandths.
Eighth of a rupee ...	Ten thousandths ...	

Copper.—Half *tanga*, weighing 200 grains troy, and corresponding with the double pice or half-anna of British India;

Quarter *tanga*, weighing 100 grains troy, and corresponding with the pice of British India;

Eighth of a *tanga*, weighing 50 grains troy, and corresponding with the half-pice of British India;

Real, or twelfth of a *tanga*, corresponding with the pie of British India.

In the making of copper coins, a remedy shall be allowed not exceeding one-fortieth in weight.

The value in copper of one Portuguese rupee will be sixteen Portuguese *tangas*, sixty-four quarter *tangas* or pices, or one hundred and ninety-two *reaes* or pies.

3. The Portuguese silver and copper coins established by this Convention shall be issued by the authority of the Government of Portuguese India, and shall be coined on behalf of the said Government by the Government of British India, and by no other agency whatever.

The Governor General of Portuguese India engages that, while this Convention continues in force, no coins other than those established by this Convention shall be coined in or imported into Portuguese India.

4. With the view of obtaining in the shortest possible time the desired uniformity of coinage throughout the respective Indian possessions of the High

Contracting Parties, the Governor General of British India engages that the Government of British India shall—

(a) forego, for the period of three years from the date on which this Convention comes into force, all duty or other charge for melting, cutting, refining or recoining any coin of the existing Portuguese Indian silver currency tendered for recoinage into Portuguese Indian coin;

(b) deliver, for the period of five years from the date of this Convention, copper coins of the Portuguese copper currency established by this Convention in exchange for copper coins of the existing Portuguese Indian copper currency which may be brought to the said mint for the purpose of such exchange, at the value represented by such last-mentioned coins in the existing Portuguese currency. The relative representative value of the old and new coin to be thus exchanged on equal terms and without charge for manufacture, shall, if the Governor General of Portuguese India so desires, be determined, once for all, by a mixed commission appointed in the manner provided in the sixteenth article of the above-cited Treaty.

(c) advance to the Governor General of Portuguese India, in the Portuguese currency established by this Convention, such sums in such denominations of coin and in such instalments (if any), as the said Governor General of Portuguese India may require; provided

1stly.—That the amount of such advances outstanding at any time shall not exceed in the whole ten lakhs of rupees.

2ndly.—That an interval of two months shall be allowed for compliance with any such requisition, and that no such advance shall be made after the expiration of eighteen months from the date on which this Convention comes into force.

3rdly.—That every such advance shall be, within two months, repaid in coin of the existing Portuguese Indian currency, equivalent thereto in intrinsic value ascertained upon assay at Her Majesty's Mint, or in copper coin of the existing Portuguese Indian currency valued as prescribed in clause (b).

5. The Governor General of British India engages that the Government of British India shall—

(a) on presentation by or on behalf of the Governor General of Portuguese India of any silver bullion or coin at the Mint at Bombay, or at such other Mint as the said Government from time to time appoints, deliver to the said Governor General or his agent, after such interval as in the judgment of the Mint Master is necessary for the process of coinage, the produce of such silver bullion or coin, in the silver coin established by this Convention, subject, always, to the same duty, charges, fees and regulations as are for the time being in force for the conversion into British Indian currency of bullion and coin presented at the said Mint: provided that, save as provided in clause 4, the said Government shall not be bound thus to deliver more than four lakhs of rupees in any one year;

(b) coin for the Governor General of Portuguese India the copper coins established by this Convention, to such amounts and in such denominations as the said Governor General may require, upon payment of the value inscribed upon such coins in the silver coin established by this Convention or in British Indian rupees: provided that, saving as engaged in clause 4, the said Government shall not be bound thus to coin more than twenty thousand rupees worth of such coin in any one year.

In lieu of any seigniorage or profits which the Portuguese Government might otherwise claim on account of the coinage on their behalf provided by this clause, the Governor General of British India engages to pay the Governor General of Portuguese India an indemnity of four thousand rupees per annum, commencing from the first day of November, one thousand eight hundred and eighty-three, and continuing as long as this Convention remains in force.

6. All silver and copper Portuguese coins, coined under the provisions of this Convention, shall, while this Convention remains in force, be legal tender in payment or on account throughout British India to the same extent, and subject to the same exceptions in the case of coin which has been called in, or is under weight, or has been clipped, filed or defaced, as in the case of the corresponding silver and copper coins issued by the authority of the Government of British India for the time being in British India.

All silver and copper coin which has been issued by the authority of the Government of British India shall, to the said same extent and subject to the same exceptions, be a legal tender in payment or on account, throughout Portuguese India.

7. The Governor General of Portuguese India agrees that, if at any time while this Convention continues in force, the Government of British India should recall the whole body of British Indian coin corresponding to any description of Portuguese coin issued under this Convention, or change the monetary system of British India, he will, if requested by such Government so to do, recall all Portuguese coin of that description, or change in like manner as the case may be, the monetary system of Portuguese India: provided that the expense incurred in recalling such coin or making such change shall be defrayed by the Government of British India.

8. When any silver coin, purporting to have been issued under the provisions of this Convention, is tendered to any officer of the Government of British India, authorized by that Government to act under this clause, and is deemed by such officer to be counterfeit, or to have been reduced in weight otherwise than by reasonable wearing, he may, by himself or another (subject to the rules which the said Government prescribes in this behalf), cut or break such coin and return the pieces to the person tendering the same, and the loss caused by such cutting and breaking shall be borne by such person.

9. When any such silver coin which has been called in is tendered to any officer of the Government of British India authorized by that Government to act under this clause, he may cut or break such coin, and shall receive it at the rate of one rupee per tola: but the expense thus incurred shall, except

when such coin has been recalled under clause 7, be borne by the Portuguese Government.

10. In like manner, when any British Indian coin which has been called in is tendered to any officer of the Government of Portuguese India authorized by that Government to act under this clause, he may cut or break such coin, and shall receive it at the rate of one rupee per tola, and the expense so incurred shall be borne by the Government of British India.

11. The Governor General of Portuguese India engages to appoint an officer who will receive, while this Convention continues in force, from any person tendering the coin next hereinafter mentioned, all silver coin issued under this Convention which may have lost, by reasonable wearing, more than two per cent., and shall pay for the same at the rate of one rupee per tola.

12. Nothing in this Convention shall be held to limit the powers of His Most Faithful Majesty the King of Portugal and the Algarves to establish at any time such system of paper currency as he may deem fit.

The Governor General of Portuguese India has the power for the present to issue the following paper money :—

Five-rupee notes, payable in copper.
Ten-rupee notes, payable in silver.

Twenty	do.	do.
Fifty	do.	do.
One hundred	do.	do.
Five hundred	do.	do.

The amount of paper money issued will never be above four per cent. of the value of the money in circulation, the Portuguese India Government notes being guaranteed by the Portuguese Government and payable to the bearer.

13. The Governor General of Portuguese India engages that, whenever the Government of British India exercises in respect of British India generally, or of all the territories adjacent to Portuguese India, the powers conferred on it under a certain Act of the Governor General of British India in Council, called 'The Indian Weights and Measures of Capacity Act, 1871,' then he the said Governor General of Portuguese India will enforce throughout Portuguese India provisions similar to those of that Act.

14. This Convention shall come into force on the first day of November, one thousand eight hundred and eighty, and shall remain in force until the expiration of a year counting from the day on which one or other of the Contracting Parties shall have given notice to the other of its intention to put an end to it; provided that no such notice shall be given until four years after the date on which the Convention comes into force.

15. The Governor General of Portuguese India undertakes that, in the event of this Convention being put an end to under clause 14 or otherwise, no coins resembling any of the coins struck under this Convention shall be struck in or imported into Portuguese India, or shall be struck under the authority of, or with the sanction of, His Most Faithful Majesty in any other place.

Done at Pangim on the twelfth day of April one thousand eight hundred and eighty.

(Sd.) CAETANO ALDRE. D'ALMEIDA ALBUQUERQUE,

Governor General of Portuguese India.

Done at Calcutta on the eighteenth day March one thousand eight hundred and eighty.

(Sd.) LYTTON,

Viceroy and Governor General of British India.

I need not describe, after this, the two following specimens of this new silver and copper coinage. (See Plate IX., figs. 10 and 11.) I may add, however, that the dies for small silver pieces of the new device intended for circulation in the Portuguese territories in India, prepared at the Calcutta mint, in conformity with the provision of the new treaty, were eventually sent to the Bombay mint, where the coins have since then been struck off. Another circumstance worth noting is that the Goa rupees and other new Indo-Portuguese coins were directed to be treated as legal tender in British India, in pursuance of the article six of the above cited Convention, which acquired the force of law within British India by Act XVII. of 1881.

The new coinage was not issued without opposition. Some thought it more patriotic to have the colonial coinage struck in the National mint at Lisbon, instead of striking it in the foreign mints of Calcutta and Bombay; others said that it would be preferable to do away with the colonial coinage altogether, and to send the Portuguese money current throughout the kingdom, to be put in circulation in the settlements abroad. But both economically and politically the system now adopted,—for at last good sense prevailed—is the most profitable to the country. I do not really know how one's patriotism lay dormant, while for years the little settlement of Damão allowed the coinage of the native princes around to circulate freely in its territory, but forbade the Goa money to pass current. Even after the new Convention money was in circulation, a clamour was raised on account of the loss entailed on the withdrawal and recoinage of worn-out and uncurrent coins; while this loss I believe did not amount to more than the usual expense of mintage everywhere, the bulk of receipts being the seignorage duty of 2 per cent on the coinage of rupees. But the greatest gain one ever extracted from this Convention is the substitution of a beautiful piece of money as a work of art, for the barbarous, irregular, ill-impressed coinage of former years.

But to return to the new coinage, it appears that 4 lacs of rupees were coined at the Calcutta mint in 1880-81 under this Monetary Convention with the Government of Portuguese India, the rest being coined at Bombay. I am indebted to Dr. Graham of the Bombay Mint for the following extract:—"The old Portuguese Indian coin, valued at Rs. 9,97,034, was received at the Bombay mint for coinage under the Monetary Convention with the Government of Portuguese India, and the value of the silver coin struck for the Goa Government during the year was Rs. 9,61,786, which is included in the total coinage of the Bombay mint."*

With regard to the copper money coined in the Bombay mint during the government of Viscount of S. Januario, or in the year 1871, the following is the catalogue of coins, with their nomenclature, number and value:—

Tangas	51,114	The value of this coinage in xerafins was:—20,837 : 1 : 47, or in Provincial reis 6,251,207.
Half Tangas	50,063	
Quarter Tangas	50,664	
Ten Reis	51,175	
Five Reis	50,900	
Three Reis	52,189	

This coinage was sent in circulation by the Resolution of the Board of Public Finance, dated the 29th of September 1871, to begin from the 1st of December following.†

To the above list I may add the two following tables of money in gold, silver, and copper, issued from the Goa mint from 1775 to 1856. It is indeed very interesting; and my only regret is that I could not succeed in getting a similar list from the day of conquest of Goa in 1510 to 1775. The two lists are as follows:—

---

* Proceedings of the Government of India, Department of Finance and Commerce—Accounts and Finance (Mint). Resolution No. 401, dated the 22nd of January 1882.

† For the above note I am indebted to Mr. J. Gracias of the Secretariat, and to Mr. J. M. do Carmo Nazareth of the Board of Public Finance of Goa. Cf. *Boletim do Governo*, No. 93 of 1871.)

Years.	Gold.	Silver.	Copper.	Seignorage.
	Marks.	Marks.	Arrobas of 32 lbs.	
1773	145	223	3,564	696
1776	261	4,098	74,434	12,193
1777	602	661	23,278	4,106
1778	62	70	......	69
1779	641	5,382	......	1,589
1780	156	2,210	......	567
1781	593	5,547	......	1,584
1782	235	3,444	......	879
1783	433	5,744	......	1,495
1784	434	6,326	......	1,612
1785	405	4,246	......	1,173
1786	243	12,016	8,429	2,598
1787	393	12,514	......	3,781
1788	90	983	......	268
1789	290	1,301	6.667	492
1790	135	1,413	......	1,391
1791	452	9,531	......	2,288
1792	426	7,556	......	1,852
1793	759	2,749	......	1,159
1794	274	1,757	......	570
1795	441	442	......	450
1796	432	1,196	25,600	585
1797	75	1,993	......	4,299
1798	29	6,907	......	1,582
1799	256	11,733	......	2,552
1800	140	10,275	19,200	2,167
1801	12	2,937	6,420	3,477
1802	163	1,099	......	1,503

Years.	GOLD.							SILVER.							COPPER.		
	Weight.				Value.			Weight.				Value.			Weight.		Value.
	Marks.	oz.	drs.	grs.	xerafins.	tgs.	reis.	Marks.	oz.	drs.	grs.	xerafins.	tgs.	reis.	Arrobas.	lbs. oz. drs.	xerafins. tgs. reis.
1803	196	4	3	45	111,838	3	35	3,571	3	7	06	150,487	2	43	...	......	....
1804	580	2	6	02	330,489	2	54	10,638	2	7	00	393,810	0	45	...	......	....
1805	342	4	1	32	117,220	3	39	11,165	2	4	00	470,463	1	45	...	......	....
1806	158	2	1	16	89,758	1	33	7,231	0	2	00	299,976	4	34	...	......	....
1807	76	3	4	47	42,487	2	11	10,290	5	6	24	371,758	3	28	...	......	....
1808	132	2	4	11	72,473	4	05	3,363	7	2	60	140,702	1	26	...	......	....
1809	124	0	1	55	71,615	3	35	1,487	3	1	12	52,526	4	54	...	......	....
1810	72	7	1	29	41,417	1	09	513	4	2	00	21,605	4	29	...	......	....
1811	94	6	1	25	52,893	3	44	4,492	1	0	00	186,330	0	20	...	......	....
1812	105	7	7	34	60,222	0	06	2,413	5	2	48	101,182	0	49	...	......	....
1813	172	3	4	44	80,053	0	35	856	6	2	60	14,665	0	16	...	......	....
1814	243	3	0	44	138,762	4	54	1,015	0	6	63	43,248	0	46	...	......	....
1815	152	0	6	41	86,384	2	00	562	3	0	60	23,571	2	06	...	......	....
1816	83	2	0	39	47,199	4	25	4,027	2	2	36	168,684	1	43	...	......	....
1817	176	1	0	14	71,605	1	14	1,403	1	6	60	62,641	2	49	...	......	....
1818	96	2	5	34	53,099	2	02	1,527	2	6	24	66,028	2	46	...	......	....
1819	60	2	0	12	35,044	2	57	1,461	6	6	48	61,596	2	24	...	......	....
1820	31	2	3	16	17,758	3	03	1,369	1	5	12	58,078	1	25	...	......	....
1821	43	7	1	41	24,884	0	41	289	2	7	24	12,129	1	07	...	......	....
1822	24	5	7	20	12,927	4	23	529	1	6	48	22,192	4	05	...	......	....
1823	15	1	7	40	8,599	3	12	1,217	5	6	60	50,920	2	20	...	......	....
1824	24	5	0	36	14,010	3	04	1,098	3	6	30	46,041	4	00	...	......	....
1825	29	1	4	06	15,723	2	34	4,801	3	3	24	201,508	0	49	...	......	....
1826	61	0	4	36	34,734	2	29	992	5	1	18	36,776	2	38	...	......	....
1827	10	4	0	00	6,114	2	05	1,458	4	0	37	61,155	2	01	...	......	....
1828	4	6	4	00	2,737	1	28	2,927	5	4	56	125,961	3	01	...	......	....
1829	1	1	0	00	640	4	24	979	0	7	00	35,179	2	37	...	......	....

1830	11	2	2	00	6,416	2	39	671	5	4	12	24,987	1	24	...	......			....		
1831	......	......			....			757	5	3	00	31,768	3	45	...	......			....		
1832	......	......			....			200	1	0	00	8,635	3	31	...	......			....		
1833	3	1	4	00	1,812	2	43	257	4	0	00	7,087	4	13	...	......			....		
1834	......	......			....			54	6	4	00	2,306	4	22	...	......			....		
1838	......	......			....			123	2	5	00	4,180	0	40	...	......			....		
1839	......	......			....			3,470	0	4	36	157,455	3	28	...	......			....		
1840	29	0	6	12	16,669	3	12	905	1	0	36	36,766	0	37	...	......			....		
1841	20	3	1	00	11,742	1	35	195	5	3	00	8,189	0	16	...	......			....		
1845	......	......			....			9,937	0	3	20	436,220	0	36	42	15	11	5	2,889	2	35
1846	......	......			....			9,101	6	0	00	400,474	3	16	28	24	00	0	1,876	0	00
1847	......	......			....			54	6	3	36	2,306	1	08	10	11	1	0	873	2	30
1848	......	......			....			8,251	3	5	62	334,175	2	34	5	00	12	0	337	1	16
1849	......	......			....			1,635	0	5	40	66,217	4	27	...	......			....		
1850	......	......			....			52	5	7	00	2,109	1	55	59	21	8	0	8,989	3	42
1851	......	......			....			395	0	0	43	8,272	2	36	70	31	6	0	4,770	2	28
1852	......	......			....			......	......			....			199	3	00	2	13,418	3	00
1853	......	......			....			......	......			....			54	00	00	4	3,639	4	15
1854	......	......			....			......	......			....			45	24	12	2	3,064	1	12
1855	......	......			....			......	......			....			...	......			....		
1856	......	......			....			......	......			....			9	20	7	0	775	2	45

Lastly we have the following short list of money coined at Goa and at Diu from the 13th of August 1856 to the end of December 1869, when the mint was for ever closed.

	Marks.	oz.	drms.	grs.	Value. Xerafins.	Tanga.	Reis.
Money coined for the State of Goa ..	1,185	3	2	6	52,748	3	22
Do. for the Settlement of Diu.	119	5	1	58½	7,254	3	56
Do. for private persons	58,038	1	4	36	2,488	097	2·09

It is evident from the above that for some years the Diu mint remained closed, money for that place being coined at Goa.

Private individuals had the privilege to send bullion to the mint, receiving in return coin, after paying the cost of mintage and the seignorage.

The tables and the lists above given show clearly that the mint of Goa was in active operation continuously from 1775 to 1802, then from that year to 1856, with only two short interruptions—from 1835 to 1837, and from 1842 to 1844. Then again it was in uninterrupted activity from 1856 to the end of 1869, when the mint, which was first opened in 1510, was declared extinct. Now the Bombay mint in 1871 issued copper coin for the territories of Portuguese India, and finally both Calcutta and Bombay mints from 1880 to 1882 under the Monetary Convention quoted above. The amount of the copper money coined under the Convention is not yet known, as the withdrawal of the old copper coin from circulation is not yet completed.*

Carlos Eugenio de Almeida.

This Governor General of Portuguese India, whose number is 128th in the catalogue from D. Francisco de Almeida, the first viceroy of India, who was appointed on the 24th of October 1505, assumed charge of his office in April 1882. He has published some resolutions relating to the withdrawal of old coin and distribution of the new. The time allowed for withdrawing old copper coin ends in October 1883, but it may be prolonged, as was the case with old silver coins.

It remains now to describe two pattern pieces, one dated 1834, and the other 1862.

---

* For the proportion or ratio between the old and new reis, see Supp. No. 115 of the *Bol. Off. do Gov. do Estado da India*, of the 16th of October 1880.

Obv.—The coat-of-arms of the kingdom, having on each side three series of points in the form of a cross, and the legend RUPIA DE GOA round the margin.

Rev.—A star, 600, and R. in three lines in the field inside a wreath of oak and laurel, and the year 1834 in the exergue. Silver. *Rupia.* Weight, 171 grains Troy. (See Plate IX., fig. 12.)

Of this coinage there were also struck the sub-divisions of xerafim, of two different types, and meio xerafim also of two different designs. There was also a copper coinage of one of these types, consisting of the tanga and its fractions of half, 10, 5, and 3 reis. The other pattern piece was as follows :—

Obv.—The coat-of-arms of the kingdom, the marginal legend LUDOVICUS I. PORTUG. ET ALGAR. REX., and the year 1862.

Rev.—RUPIA-GOA-600 REIS in three lines within a crown of laurel. Silver. *Rupia.* Weight, 167 grains Troy. (See Plate IX., fig. 13.)

Only the rupee was issued. None of these coins, although of far better workmanship, were sent in circulation, on account of objections raised against their weight, and their not conforming with the standard and fractional system of the old coinage. In short it was the spirit of conservatism in opposition to all innovation. The two specimens above described, as well the two drawn at Plate VI., figs. 8 and 9, belong to the collection of Mr. J. M. de Souza Brito, ex-factor of the now extinct Factory of Surat.

Having concluded the subject of coinages, I pass on to sketch a short history of the Portuguese mints in the East. I have already mentioned that the mints of Malacca, Colombo, and Cochin, established soon after the conquest, were forcibly abolished on the capture of those settlements by the Dutch. Those to the north of Goa, viz. :— Diu, Daman, Bassein and Chaul had a different fate. The Chaul mint was probably established in 1664, and in 1667, by a resolution of the Government in Council, foreign copper and tutenag money was prohibited circulation there, as well as at Daman and Bassein with their dependencies. It was closed on its cession to the Marâṭhâs in 1740. The Daman and Bassein mints, opened between 1609 and 1612 for the issue of copper bazaruccos, and later on of the tutenag ones, were closed in 1739, on the capture of Bassein. The Daman Mint was however, opened again in 1842 for the issue of copper tangas and their sub-divisions, and was closed again within a decade. It has since then been abolished.

The Diu mint was, from its foundation about the middle of the seventeenth century, kept open until perhaps 1856, when it seems its materials and machinery were transferred to Goa, where money was struck for circulation in that settlement.

The Goa mint-house, situated at a street behind the bishop's palace in the early days of the conquest, was in 1552 placed inside the Fort, and in 1589 was transferred to the Gunpowder Factory at Panelim, where it remained for a short time, and was eventually removed to the *Ribeira Grande* in the city. It was again carried back to Panelim, and from this place to Pangim in 1834. In 1842 the whole establishment was sent to the arsenal in the old city, where it remained until the extinction of the arsenal, decreed on the 25th of November 1869. Such are the vicissitudes undergone by the Goa mint from its foundation in 1510 to its extinction in 1869.

It is a matter for reflection that the Portuguese, who only about a hundred and fifty years ago were still powerful to the extent of Lord Clive using the Portuguese language as his only medium of communication with the native princes,* and of the Bombay Government imitating the Portuguese currency, as shown above, should now in their turn adopt the British system of coinage, and even have their money struck in the British mints. This change of fortune reminds me of that learned Goa financier and Latinist, who having been requested by the viceroy to express his opinion on the exchange of *bazaruccos*, and its variable character, a subject I have already alluded to, replied, among other quotations, with the following :—" *Quisquis habet nummos secura naviget aura, Fortunamque suo temperet arbitrio.*" The poverty of Portugal and of her colonies, it seems, has more than anything else contributed to the closing of all her mints in India, and signing a Monetary Convention whereby Portugal has certainly lost one of those privileges, which all nations highly appreciate, viz., striking their own money. But this has been a necessity of her economical position in the world, and the best solution of the financial problem the Portuguese Government had for years strived in vain to solve.

Of the once vast dominion of the Portuguese in the East, all monuments, whether edifices, or archives, are rapidly disappearing. The

---

* Life of Lord Clive. See *Academy* of the 10th of September 1881.

only documents that will longer defy the action of time are coins. To them I have devoted my attention, which has resulted in this first attempt in a foreign language, to write the history of the Portuguese in India by means of coins ; for in the case of the Portuguese, more perhaps than in that of any other modern nation, one may safely apply the trite saying of Ovid, the motto of some Numismatic Societies—*Factum abiit—monumenta manent.* In conclusion, I append below the words of Swift on the usefulness and authenticity of coins as historical documents :—" of undoubted authority, of necessary use and observation, not perishable by time, nor confined to any certain place ; properties not to be found in books, statues, pictures, buildings or any other monuments of illustrious actions."